THE WOK
COOKBOOK
How to cook just about anything in a wok

THE WOK
COOKBOOK

How to cook just about anything in a wok

Crescent Books
New York

©1988 Ottenheimer Publishers, Inc.
This 1988 edition is published by Ottenheimer
Publishers, Inc. for Crescent Books,
distributed by Crown Publishers, Inc., 225 Park
Avenue South, New York, New York, 10003.
All Rights Reserved
Printed in Hong Kong

Library of Congress Cataloging-in-Publication Data

Passmore, Jacki.
    Wok cookbook.

    Includes index.
    1. Wok cookery.   I. Title.
TX840.W65P37   1988   641.5′8   87-13605
ISBN 0-517-64756-7

h g f e d c b a

Contents

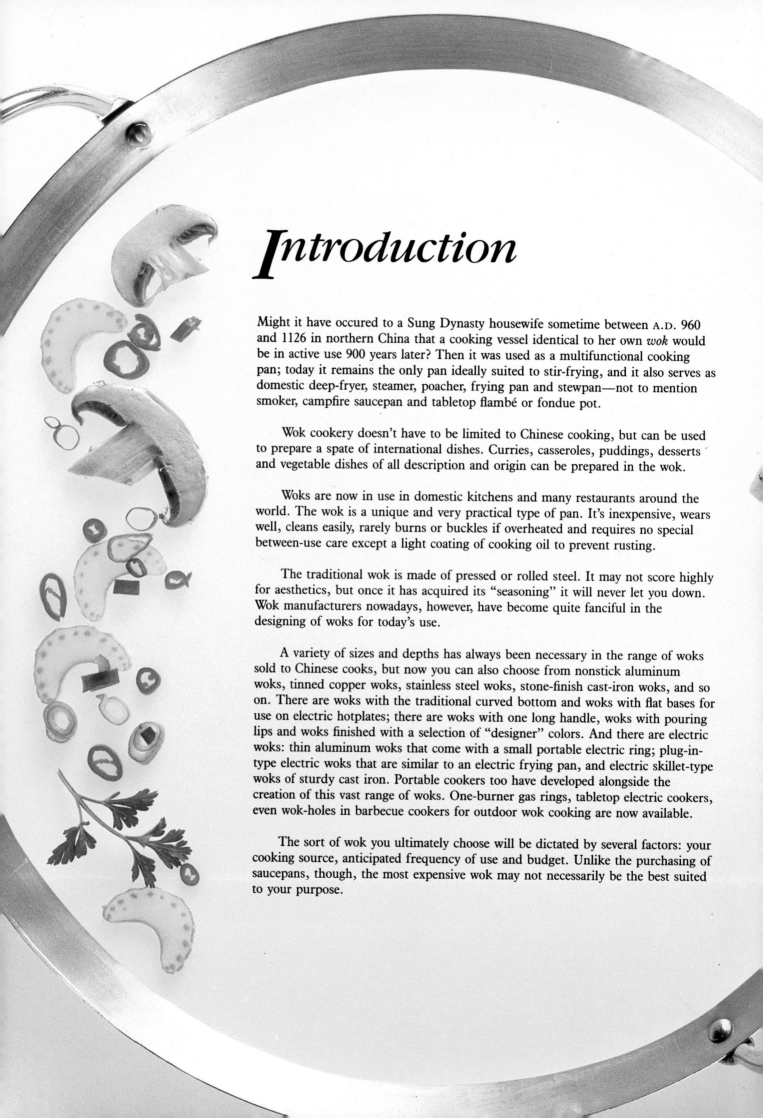

*I*ntroduction

Might it have occured to a Sung Dynasty housewife sometime between A.D. 960 and 1126 in northern China that a cooking vessel identical to her own *wok* would be in active use 900 years later? Then it was used as a multifunctional cooking pan; today it remains the only pan ideally suited to stir-frying, and it also serves as domestic deep-fryer, steamer, poacher, frying pan and stewpan—not to mention smoker, campfire saucepan and tabletop flambé or fondue pot.

Wok cookery doesn't have to be limited to Chinese cooking, but can be used to prepare a spate of international dishes. Curries, casseroles, puddings, desserts and vegetable dishes of all description and origin can be prepared in the wok.

Woks are now in use in domestic kitchens and many restaurants around the world. The wok is a unique and very practical type of pan. It's inexpensive, wears well, cleans easily, rarely burns or buckles if overheated and requires no special between-use care except a light coating of cooking oil to prevent rusting.

The traditional wok is made of pressed or rolled steel. It may not score highly for aesthetics, but once it has acquired its "seasoning" it will never let you down. Wok manufacturers nowadays, however, have become quite fanciful in the designing of woks for today's use.

A variety of sizes and depths has always been necessary in the range of woks sold to Chinese cooks, but now you can also choose from nonstick aluminum woks, tinned copper woks, stainless steel woks, stone-finish cast-iron woks, and so on. There are woks with the traditional curved bottom and woks with flat bases for use on electric hotplates; there are woks with one long handle, woks with pouring lips and woks finished with a selection of "designer" colors. And there are electric woks: thin aluminum woks that come with a small portable electric ring; plug-in-type electric woks that are similar to an electric frying pan, and electric skillet-type woks of sturdy cast iron. Portable cookers too have developed alongside the creation of this vast range of woks. One-burner gas rings, tabletop electric cookers, even wok-holes in barbecue cookers for outdoor wok cooking are now available.

The sort of wok you ultimately choose will be dictated by several factors: your cooking source, anticipated frequency of use and budget. Unlike the purchasing of saucepans, though, the most expensive wok may not necessarily be the best suited to your purpose.

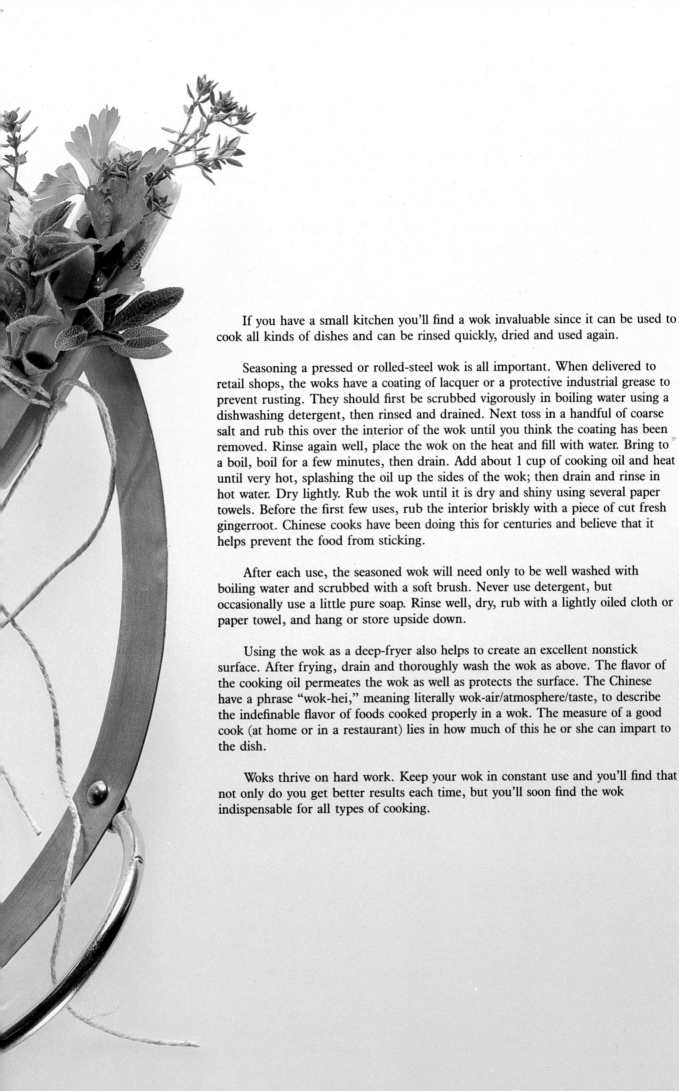

If you have a small kitchen you'll find a wok invaluable since it can be used to cook all kinds of dishes and can be rinsed quickly, dried and used again.

Seasoning a pressed or rolled-steel wok is all important. When delivered to retail shops, the woks have a coating of lacquer or a protective industrial grease to prevent rusting. They should first be scrubbed vigorously in boiling water using a dishwashing detergent, then rinsed and drained. Next toss in a handful of coarse salt and rub this over the interior of the wok until you think the coating has been removed. Rinse again well, place the wok on the heat and fill with water. Bring to a boil, boil for a few minutes, then drain. Add about 1 cup of cooking oil and heat until very hot, splashing the oil up the sides of the wok; then drain and rinse in hot water. Dry lightly. Rub the wok until it is dry and shiny using several paper towels. Before the first few uses, rub the interior briskly with a piece of cut fresh gingerroot. Chinese cooks have been doing this for centuries and believe that it helps prevent the food from sticking.

After each use, the seasoned wok will need only to be well washed with boiling water and scrubbed with a soft brush. Never use detergent, but occasionally use a little pure soap. Rinse well, dry, rub with a lightly oiled cloth or paper towel, and hang or store upside down.

Using the wok as a deep-fryer also helps to create an excellent nonstick surface. After frying, drain and thoroughly wash the wok as above. The flavor of the cooking oil permeates the wok as well as protects the surface. The Chinese have a phrase "wok-hei," meaning literally wok-air/atmosphere/taste, to describe the indefinable flavor of foods cooked properly in a wok. The measure of a good cook (at home or in a restaurant) lies in how much of this he or she can impart to the dish.

Woks thrive on hard work. Keep your wok in constant use and you'll find that not only do you get better results each time, but you'll soon find the wok indispensable for all types of cooking.

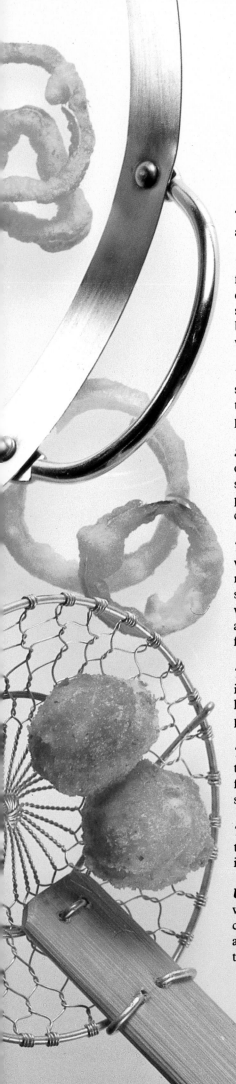

Wok Accessories

There are a number of simple utensils and accessories that are used with the wok, and which will be required for different recipes in this book.

The wok "charn" is a flat lifting instrument, similar to a spatula but with its front edge slightly curved to allow it to follow the interior curve of the wok. The charn is used as the manipulating utensil during stir-frying, but also doubles as a spoon for lifting, stirring, mixing and breaking up ingredients in the pan. It will be necessary to acquire a wooden spatula to use (instead of a metal "charn") with woks that have a nonstick lining.

The steamer rack is a metal or bamboo rack, shaped to fit inside the wok to support the food to be cooked, either by itself or in a dish, above the bottom of the wok. There should be sufficient space below the rack for water to boil to produce the steam.

Steaming baskets are circular baskets of tightly woven cane or bamboo with their own close-fitting lids. They are used for cooking Chinese dim-sum and other steamed dishes. The metal basket-shaped or flat perforated inserts supplied with a pressure cooker can be used in place of steamer racks or steamer baskets. These can also be used as the support for fish during poaching.

The draining rack/ladle is a perforated metal or wire rack/ladle (skimmer) on which deep-fried foods are rested to drain off excess oil. Ladles can be used to retrieve the food directly from the oil. If unobtainable, use a slotted (perforated) spoon. Draining can also be done on paper towels. Some woks come equipped with a draining rack, which clips on the inside rim of the wok. These are acceptable, but the food should not be left on them for a long time as the steam from the dish will cause the crisp surface to soften.

The wok lid is used for steaming, poaching, braising and smoking, and in some instances during sautéeing. Without a dome-shaped lid, your wok would be only half-efficient. If your wok is not equipped with a lid, use a large saucepan lid or plate.

The wok stand is a perforated metal ring or wire molded rack on which to stand the wok between uses. It is particularly useful if the wok is to be used for deep-frying, because the full wok of hot oil can be placed safely out of danger on a work surface after use.

The wok ladle is more like an overgrown spoon than a soup ladle; it is used by the Chinese cook as an all-purpose measuring spoon, mixing bowl for sauce ingredients, tasting spoon, and so on. A soup ladle will suffice.

Useful extras include a sturdy but soft scrubbing brush for brushing out the wok during washing; a pair of large wooden cooking chopsticks; a good cleaver; a chopping board; several heatproof dishes and plates that can be used for steaming; and one or two sturdy oven gloves or pot holders. These should always be on hand to use when holding or lifting the wok.

Steamer rack

Wok charn

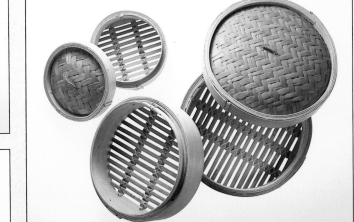

Steaming baskets

*Draining rack
and ladle*

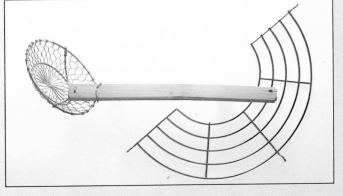

Wok and lid

*Wok brushes,
chopsticks*

Wok ladle

Wok stand

Cleaver, chopping board, oven gloves

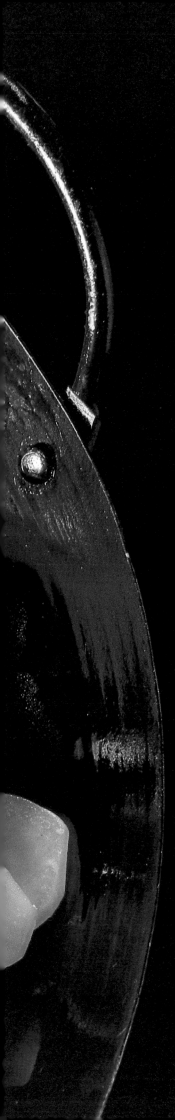

Stir-frying and Sautéeing

Stir-frying is an energetic and enjoyable cooking method involving active participation from the cook. The wok—although developed by the Chinese as their basic cooking vessel—can be considered as the only really suitable pan for the rapid cooking and constant manipulation that is required for stir-frying. Its uniquely shaped interior allows a smooth sweep across the inside by its accompanying "charn," which has a curved edge designed to follow the curve of the wok. The rounded bottom of the wok means that it can sit closely over the heat source—particularly over a gas ring—with the heat being distributed evenly up the sides of the pan.

The wok should be well heated before cooking begins, then the cooking medium (vegetable oil, lard or chicken fat) added and heated until a blue haze filling the interior of the wok indicates that it is ready. At this point, the food is tossed into the pan and vigorously stirred with the charn. Because the handles of most woks heat up quickly, wear a sturdy protective glove on the left hand to hold the wok steady, and manipulate the charn with the right hand. The action is fast and continuous: tossing, turning, flipping, stirring, and occasionally shaking the wok with the left hand to aid in the unceasing movements of the wok's contents. Foods to be stir-fried should be prepared in advance and assembled together with the required seasoning and sauce ingredients in the cooking area.

As most Chinese stir-fried dishes include a variety of meats and vegetables, it may be necessary to cook these in several batches. Once one lot is done, remove it deftly with the charn to a warmed plate; add the remaining ingredients as dictated by the recipe, cook, then bring the components together.

Sautéeing differs little from stir-frying. Again the ingredients are usually cut into small pieces for quick cooking. Once sautéed and browned on both sides, the ingredients may be removed from the pan and kept warm while the sauce is prepared.

Whereas stir-frying employs mainly vegetable oil as its cooking medium, butter or a mixture of butter and cooking oil are used for sautéeing. Some or all of this fat is generally drained off before the pan is deglazed with wine or liquor, which bubble up and draw off anything that may have stuck to the bottom of the pan, thus creating the basis for the sauce. This is then thickened, enriched with cream or egg yolks or thinned with stock according to the recipe requirements. The meat may be returned to the pan to be warmed through, but on no account should it be allowed to boil in its sauce or it will toughen.

The sauté method, to achieve perfection, should be done at the very last minute and the food served immediately on warmed plates. There should be enough room in the pan to allow space between the pieces of meat or they begin to steam and stew instead of quickly sealing and browning. Yet at the same time, there should be enough ingredients in the pan to temper the heat of the fat, which should never be allowed to burn or it will impart a bitter taste to the sauce.

The wok performs most acceptably as a sauté pan. Foods can cover the bottom and extend partially up the smooth sides of the pan where the heat will be maintained evenly. In fact, the flat-based woks now being produced for use on electric cookers are not at all dissimilar to the traditional French sauté pan, the *sautoir*.

Garlic Shrimp

SERVES 6

2 pounds large uncooked shrimp in the shell
¾ cup good olive oil
6 to 7 cloves garlic, sliced
1 fresh red chili, sliced
6 fresh basil leaves (optional)
Salt

Wash the shrimp and dry them with paper towels. Heat the oil in the wok and sauté the garlic and chili briefly. Add the shrimp, and cook on moderate to high heat until the shells turn a bright pink and the shrimp are cooked through (about 3 minutes). Add the basil leaves and salt.

Transfer to heated ramekins or other small dishes and pour on the oil from the pan. Serve piping hot, with crusty bread and lemon wedges.

Squid Provençale

SERVES 6

This versatile dish can be adapted for scallops, shrimp or other seafood, or served as a main course.

1 pound cleaned squid
1 large onion
1 clove garlic
1¼ pounds tomatoes
1 tablespoon butter
1 tablespoon olive oil
1 bay leaf
½ teaspoon dried sage or basil
½ teaspoon sugar
Salt and black pepper
2 teaspoons parsley, chopped

Wash squid, dry and cut into rings. Peel and finely chop the onion and garlic. Plunge the tomatoes into a saucepan of boiling water and remove at the count of eight; peel, then chop roughly.

Heat the wok and add the butter and olive oil. When hot, add the squid and sauté until it just turns white; then remove and keep warm. Add the onion and garlic to the wok and sauté gently until lightly browned. Add the tomatoes and cook on moderate heat for 7 minutes, adding the bay leaf, the sage or basil,

Toss shrimp in hot oil until they turn pink

Pour garlic-flavored oil over shrimp and serve

the sugar and seasonings. Return the squid to the wok and stir in the chopped parsley. Heat through and serve at once. The squid should not be overcooked or it will toughen.

Wash and dry squid, then cut into rings

Plunge tomatoes into boiling water, then peel

Sauté squid in olive oil and butter in wok

Return squid to tomato mixture in wok just until it heats through

Scallops in Pernod

SERVES 4 AS AN APPETIZER, 2 AS A MAIN COURSE

1 pound fresh scallops
3 tablespoons butter
1 small onion, chopped
1 tablespoon flour
¼ teaspoon powdered saffron or turmeric
½ cup dry white wine
½ cup light cream
2 tablespoons Pernod
Salt
Lemon juice
Chopped parsley

Wash the scallops. Place them in the wok with water to cover and bring quickly to a boil; drain, cover with cold water and, when cool, lift out and drain thoroughly.

Wipe out the wok. Heat the butter until bubbling and sauté the scallops until they turn white and firm, then remove and keep warm.

Add the chopped onion to the wok and sauté until transparent; then sprinkle on the flour and add the saffron or turmeric. Cook briefly before adding the wine. Stir well, then simmer until thickened and reduced. Add the cream and mix well; then add the Pernod, with salt and lemon juice to taste. Return the scallops and gently heat through in the sauce. Serve on a bed of white rice with chopped parsley.

Bring scallops to a boil in a covered wok

Add sautéed scallops to the wine sauce and heat

Sautéed Liver with Oregano

SERVES 4

1 pound calf's or lamb's liver
3 tablespoons olive oil
3 tablespoons butter
2 spring onions, chopped
2 cloves garlic, chopped
2 teaspoons fresh oregano, chopped, or ¾ teaspoon dried oregano
¾ teaspoon salt
Freshly ground black pepper
3 tablespoons dry white wine
3 tablespoons heavy cream

Thinly slice the liver, removing any skin and tubes. Cut into narrow strips. Heat the oil and butter together in the wok and sauté the liver quickly until it changes color. Add the onions, garlic, oregano, the salt and pepper, and continue to sauté until the liver is just cooked. Remove and keep warm.

Add the wine to the pan and boil briskly until reduced by half, then stir in the cream and heat through. Return the liver, toss with the sauce, and serve.

Thinly slice the liver and cut into shreds

Return the sautéed liver to wine and cream sauce

African Chicken Livers

SERVES 4

1 pound chicken livers
2 tablespoons cooking oil
1 large onion, chopped
2 cloves garlic, chopped
1 teaspoon fresh gingerroot, grated
1 tablespoon flour
2 tablespoons ground roasted peanuts
1 large tomato, peeled and chopped
6 to 8 fresh basil leaves, or ¾ teaspoon dried basil
1 cup chicken stock or water
1 teaspoon ground coriander
1 teaspoon salt
1 teaspoon fresh chili, chopped
Freshly ground black pepper
2 hard-boiled eggs

Cut the livers into bite-sized pieces. Heat the cooking oil in the wok and gently sauté the onion, garlic and ginger until lightly browned. Add the chicken livers and sauté for about 2 minutes, stirring frequently. Sprinkle on the flour and leave to brown slightly. Add the peanuts and stir in; cook briefly. Then add the chopped tomato and basil and sauté for 1 to 2 more minutes. Pour in the stock or water, add the spices, chili and seasonings; cover the wok and simmer for 5 minutes.

Peel the eggs and cut them into quarters; stir into the dish and serve.

Sauté chicken livers with onion, garlic and ginger

Chop fresh basil and peeled tomato

Kidneys with Celery and Bamboo Shoots

SERVES 4

6 lamb's kidneys
½ teaspoon salt
1 teaspoon dry sherry
½ teaspoon cornstarch
2 tablespoons canned bamboo shoots, drained
2 tablespoons cooking oil
1 spring onion, chopped
2 slices gingerroot, chopped
2 cloves garlic, chopped
1 fresh red chili, chopped (optional)
1 stick celery, diagonally sliced

Sauce
3½ tablespoons chicken stock
2 teaspoons light soy sauce
1 teaspoon dry sherry
1 teaspoon cornstarch
Salt and black pepper

Cut the kidneys in half and use kitchen scissors to trim away the fatty core. Soak in cold water for 20 minutes, then drain and cut into thin slices, discarding any skin. Mix with the salt, sherry and cornstarch and set aside for 10 minutes. Slice the bamboo shoots. Mix the sauce ingredients and set aside.

Heat about 2 tablespoons of cooking oil in the wok and stir-fry the sliced kidneys until lightly and evenly browned. Remove with a slotted spoon and keep warm. Add the onion, ginger and garlic, plus chili if used, and stir-fry for 1 minute. Then add the bamboo shoots and celery, and stir-fry together for 1 minute more. Pour in the sauce and bring to a brisk boil, then reduce the heat and return the kidneys to the wok. Cook gently until the sauce thickens.

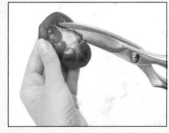

Trim fatty core from lamb's kidney

Slice the canned, drained bamboo shoots

Stir-fry sliced kidneys

Chinese Mixed Vegetables

SERVES 4

1 medium-sized carrot
1 stick celery
1 small onion
2 tablespoons canned bamboo shoots, drained
⅓ cup canned young corn cobs, drained
6 dried Chinese mushrooms, soaked
12 canned mushrooms, drained
6 canned water chestnuts, drained
1 medium Chinese cabbage (*bok choy*)
2 slices fresh gingerroot, shredded
3 tablespoons cooking oil

Sauce
3 tablespoons water or chicken stock
2 teaspoons Chinese oyster sauce
1 teaspoon dry sherry
1 teaspoon sugar
1 teaspoon cornstarch
¼ teaspoon salt

Peel and thinly slice the carrot, cutting diagonally.
String the celery if necessary and slice similarly.
Peel the onion and cut into wedges from top to root.
Thinly slice bamboo shoots and cut corn into halves.
Drain the Chinese mushrooms and remove the stems.
Cut the canned mushrooms and water chestnuts into
halves. Thoroughly wash the cabbage and chop roughly.

Heat the cooking oil in the wok and stir-fry the raw
vegetables for about 2 minutes; then add the canned vegetables
and ginger and stir-fry until just tender.

Add the sauce ingredients, premixed, and bring to a boil.
Simmer briefly and serve hot.

Thinly slice carrot and celery
diagonally

Cut onion into wedges and
then separate

Wash bok choy cabbage, then
chop roughly

Sautéed Spinach with Ham and Hazelnuts

SERVES 6

1 pound fresh spinach
2 slices smoked ham or bacon
3½ tablespoons butter
2 cloves garlic, chopped
½ teaspoon grated nutmeg
Salt
Freshly ground black pepper
3 tablespoons hazelnuts, chopped

Thoroughly wash the spinach, chop roughly and dry in a towel. Finely chop the ham or bacon and fry in the butter until crisp. Remove, drain and set aside. Add the garlic to the wok and sauté briefly; then put in the spinach and sauté, stirring frequently, for about 3 minutes. Add the nutmeg and a little salt and pepper, cover the wok and cook on moderate heat for about 5 minutes.

Remove the lid, add the ham and hazelnuts and stir on high heat until any liquid has evaporated. Serve.

Sautéed Mushrooms

SERVES 6

1 pound fresh button mushrooms
6 tablespoons butter
2 teaspoons lemon juice
Salt and black pepper
1 teaspoon lemon rind, grated
3 tablespoons fresh brown bread crumbs★
1 tablespoon parsley, chopped

Wipe mushrooms and trim the stems. Heat the butter in the wok and, when foamy, add the mushrooms; sauté over moderate heat until tender. Sprinkle on the lemon juice, and season to taste with salt and freshly ground black pepper.

Mix the lemon rind with the bread crumbs and parsley. Transfer the mushrooms to a serving plate, and sauté the crumb mixture in the remaining butter for 1 to 2 minutes; sprinkle mixture over the mushrooms and serve at once.

★Make fresh bread crumbs by placing day-old bread (crusts removed) in a blender or food processor and working briskly.

Wipe mushrooms with a damp cloth; peel if large

Sauté mushrooms in butter until tender

Wash spinach and chop roughly

Sauté spinach in butter and garlic in wok

Sprinkle lemon rind, crumbs and parsley on mushrooms

Glazed Carrots and Onions

SERVES 6

12 baby carrots
12 small (pickling) onions
1 tablespoon butter
1 tablespoon light brown sugar
Freshly ground black pepper

Scrub the carrots without peeling. Peel the onions; trim off the roots but leave the bulb of the root intact. Cut a cross in the bottom of each onion to prevent them falling apart during cooking. Boil the carrots and onions separately in salted water until tender, then drain well.

Melt the butter in the wok on low heat, then add the sugar and the vegetables. Cover and cook gently, shaking the wok from time to time to turn the vegetables, until the sugar becomes a sticky, shiny glaze. Add pepper and serve.

Stir-fried Broccoli

SERVES 6

1¼ pounds fresh broccoli
1 clove garlic, crushed
½ teaspoon sugar
3 tablespoons vegetable oil
2 teaspoons dry sherry
3 tablespoons water or chicken stock
Salt

Wash the broccoli in cold water; drain and cut into florets. Place the garlic and sugar in the wok with the vegetable oil, and heat to smoking point. Put in the broccoli and stir-fry for 2 minutes; then splash in the sherry and cook briefly. Add the water or chicken stock, cover the wok and cook on high heat for about 2 minutes, until the vegetables are just tender and most of the liquid has evaporated. Add a little salt to taste and serve at once.

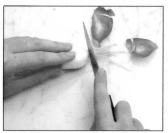
Trim roots from onions, leaving bulb intact

Cut a cross in onion to prevent falling apart

Cut the well-washed broccoli into florets

Add water to the stir-fried broccoli in wok

Toss blanched carrots and onions in butter

Sautéed Potatoes

SERVES 6

1½ pounds potatoes
3 tablespoons butter
3 tablespoons cooking oil
Salt and black pepper
2 teaspoons parsley, chopped
⅓ teaspoon fresh rosemary, chopped

Scrub the potatoes and boil in their skins in salted water until just tender. Drain, peel and slice.

Heat the butter and oil together in the wok, and slide in all the potatoes. Sprinkle on a generous amount of salt and pepper and sauté, turning occasionally, until golden.

Sprinkle on the herbs and stir in lightly, taking care not to break up the potatoes. Serve.

Sautéed sliced onion or chopped crisply fried bacon can be added for interest.

Sour Cabbage with Walnuts

SERVES 4–6

1 pound white cabbage
3 tablespoons butter
5 black peppercorns, lightly crushed
3 tablespoons walnuts, chopped
3 tablespoons white vinegar
2½ teaspoons sugar
Salt

Rinse, dry and finely shred the cabbage. Heat the butter in the wok and add the lightly crushed peppercorns and the walnuts. Sauté for 1 minute, then add the cabbage and toss until evenly coated with the butter. Sauté, stirring, for about 5 minutes until almost tender.

Add the vinegar mixed with the sugar and continue to cook and stir until the liquid has evaporated. Add salt to taste and serve.

Slice the boiled and peeled potatoes

Sprinkle fresh herbs over stir-fried potatoes

Finely shred the cabbage using a sharp knife

Add cabbage to walnuts and peppercorns in wok

Pour in vinegar and sugar and cook until evaporated

Stir-fried Beef with Vegetables

Add soy sauce and flavorings to beef

Cut chili into fine strips, discarding seeds

Return beef to stir-fried vegetables in wok

SERVES 4

½ pound fillet steak
1 tablespoon light
   soy sauce
2 teaspoons dry sherry
1 teaspoon cornstarch
½ teaspoon sugar
1 small green pepper
1 small red pepper
1 fresh red chili
1 stick celery
1 small carrot
¼ cup canned sliced
   bamboo shoots, drained
3 tablespoons cooking oil
2 slices fresh gingerroot,
   shredded

Sauce
3½ tablespoons chicken
   stock
2 to 3 teaspoons Hoisin
   sauce (sweet bean paste)
1 teaspoon dry sherry
¾ teaspoon cornstarch

Very thinly slice the beef, cutting across the grain, then cut into narrow strips. This is much more easily achieved if the meat is partially frozen. Place in a dish and add the soy sauce, sherry, cornstarch and sugar. Mix well and leave at room temperature for 20 minutes.

Trim away the inner ribs and seed pods from the peppers and chili, and cut into narrow strips. Cut the celery, carrot and bamboo shoots into julienne (matchstick) strips. Mix the sauce ingredients together in a small jug and set aside. (Make a paste of the cornstarch and some of the liquid before adding to the sauce.)

Heat the wok and add the cooking oil. Stir-fry the beef on high heat until evenly and lightly browned. Remove and keep warm.

Add the vegetables and ginger and stir-fry until they begin to soften (about 2 minutes), then pour in the sauce and boil rapidly for 30 seconds. Return the beef and continue to cook on high heat until the sauce has thickened. Serve at once.

Beef and Broccoli on Ribbon Noodles

SERVES 4

¼ pound fillet steak
1 teaspoon light soy sauce
1 teaspoon dry sherry
1 teaspoon vegetable oil
1 teaspoon cornstarch
½ teaspoon sugar
Pinch of white pepper
6 tablespoons broccoli florets
2 spring onions, shredded
2 slices fresh gingerroot, shredded
1⅔ cups fresh rice ribbon noodles
¼ cup cooking oil

Sauce
¾ cup chicken stock
2 to 3 teaspoons Chinese oyster sauce
1 teaspoon dark soy sauce
1 teaspoon dry sherry
¾ teaspoon sugar
2 teaspoons cornstarch

Cut the steak into paper-thin slices, then into strips, and place in a dish with the soy sauce, sherry, oil, cornstarch, sugar and pepper. Mix well and leave for 20 minutes.

Rinse the broccoli and drain well. Prepare the onions and ginger. Pour boiling water over noodles and stir gently until separate.

In a small bowl, mix together all the sauce ingredients except the cornstarch. Make a paste with a little of the mixture and the cornstarch; then add it to the sauce and set aside.

Heat the wok and add the cooking oil. Stir-fry the beef over high heat until lightly browned; then remove. Add the vegetables to the wok; stir-fry for about 2 minutes, then remove.

Add the noodles to the wok and stir-fry in the oil remaining in the wok until lightly (about 4 minutes). Transfer to a serving plate.

Return the vegetables to the pan and pour in the sauce. Bring to the boil, stirring. Return the meat and heat through, then pour over the noodles and serve at once.

Cut the steak into paper-thin slices

Shred ginger and onions finely

Pour boiling water over fresh rice noodles

Heat vegetables and sauce before adding meat

Orange Lamb Scallops

SERVES 4

1½ pounds leg of lamb
3 large oranges
1 tablespoon vegetable oil
3 tablespoons butter
1 small onion, grated
2 teaspoons honey
Salt and black pepper

Cut lamb into scallops

Beat each lightly with the side of a cleaver

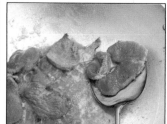

Sauté lamb in oil and butter until browned

Trim the boned lamb and cut into small, thin scallops. Beat each lightly with the side of a cleaver or a rolling pin to tenderize. Squeeze the juice from 2 oranges and finely grate the rind of 1 of them. Slice the third orange thinly and arrange the slices on a serving plate.

Heat the wok and add the oil and butter. Sauté the lamb for about 2½ minutes until evenly browned on the surface and almost cooked through. Remove and keep warm.

Add the grated onion to the wok and sauté until lightly browned. Then add the orange juice, the grated rind and the honey; bring to a boil and simmer for 1 minute. Return the lamb to the wok to simmer gently, without boiling, for about 2 minutes. Season with salt and pepper, then transfer to a serving plate and serve hot.

Flatten slices of pork with heel of hand

To crush garlic, sprinkle with salt, mash with knife

Pound pork slices with a rolling pin to flatten

Wrap a slice of pork around quartered leeks

Pork Fillets in Paprika Cream Sauce

SERVES 4–6

1 pound pork fillets
3 tablespoons butter
1 medium onion, finely chopped
1 to 2 cloves garlic, crushed
1 thick slice bacon, diced
1 small green pepper, diced
1 small red pepper, diced
1 teaspoon salt
¼ teaspoon freshly ground black pepper
1½ teaspoons sweet paprika
½ cup heavy cream

Very thinly slice the pork, then pound into small scallops. Sauté in the butter until lightly browned, then remove and keep warm.

Add the onion and garlic to the wok and sauté until beginning to brown. Add the diced bacon and sauté until crisp. Add the peppers, which have been cut into small dice, and sauté until softened (about 2 minutes). Add the remaining ingredients and bring almost to a boil. Simmer gently for 1 minute, then return the pork and heat gently in the sauce for 1 to 1½ minutes more. Serve immediately.

Pork Rolls Teriyaki

SERVES 6

6 large thin slices of leg pork (approx. 1¼ pounds)
6 small leeks or large spring onions
¼ cup dry sherry or sake
6 tablespoons sugar
¼ cup light soy sauce
3 tablespoons cooking oil
1 cucumber

Pound the pork slices lightly with a rolling pin or meat mallet to tenderize. Trim the leeks or spring onions and wash thoroughly. Wrap a slice of pork around each leek or spring onion and secure with toothpicks. Mix the sherry, sugar and soy sauce together in a small bowl.

Heat the wok and add the cooking oil. Sauté the pork rolls until lightly browned all over. Add the sauce and simmer gently until reduced to a thick and shiny glaze on the meat. Turn the rolls frequently during cooking to ensure they are evenly glazed.

Cut the cucumber into sticks or small wedges. Transfer the pork rolls to a serving plate and surround with the cucumber.

Pork Rolls Teriyaki can also be served as an appetizer. Make them smaller, using medium-sized spring onions and small thin scallops of pork, and serve one or two per person with cubes of cucumber that have been marinated in a mixture of sugar, salt and vinegar.

Sautéed Veal with Asparagus Sauce

SERVES 4–6

Asparagus gives its distinct flavor and a delicate green coloring to the purée sauce which accompanies tiny scallops of veal. Try it with fresh asparagus when in season. Or replace the cream with beaten Ricotta cheese to make a dieter's special.

1 pound veal steak
Butter for cooking
Salt and black pepper
2 spring onions, chopped
1 tablespoon flour
1 can green asparagus
3 tablespoons heavy cream
½ teaspoon lemon juice

Cut the veal into small thin scallops and pound each piece with a rolling pin or meat mallet to tenderize.

Heat about 2 tablespoons of butter in the wok and when it begins to foam, put in the veal and sauté on both sides until golden. Add the onions and sauté briefly, then sprinkle on the flour and allow to brown slightly.

Purée half the asparagus with half of the liquid from the can in a blender. Pour into the wok and bring almost to a boil. Reduce heat and simmer gently for 5 minutes. Stir in the cream and lemon juice, then transfer to a warmed serving plate.

Rinse out the wok and heat the remaining asparagus in its liquid. Drain and arrange over the meat.

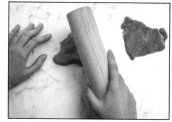
Cut veal into scallops and pound to tenderize

Sauté veal in the hot butter in wok until golden

Purée the asparagus and add to veal in the wok

Quick Chicken and Mango Curry

SERVES 2 AS A MAIN COURSE, 4 AS AN APPETIZER

½ pound chicken breasts
1 small onion, chopped
2 slices fresh gingerroot, shredded
2 tablespoons cooking oil
1½ teaspoons mild curry powder
1 tablespoon flour
½ teaspoon salt
¾ cup water or chicken stock
1 tablespoon compressed coconut cream★
4 slices fresh or canned mango
1 tablespoon toasted slivered almonds

Cut the chicken breasts into cubes after removing skin and any fragments of bone. Sauté the chicken pieces, onion, and ginger in cooking oil in the wok until the chicken is well browned and the onion soft. Sprinkle on the curry powder, flour and salt and stir; then add the water and the grated or finely chopped coconut cream. Bring almost to a boil, then reduce the heat and simmer gently, stirring, until the sauce thickens and the coconut is dissolved. Add the mango and nuts and serve on a bed of white rice.

Or use ¾ cup of canned or fresh coconut milk.

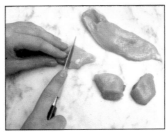

Cut the boned and skinned chicken into cubes

Finely chop the compressed coconut cream

Chicken Breasts in Green Peppercorn Sauce

SERVES 4

2 whole chicken breasts (approx. 1½ lb)
6 tablespoons butter
2 spring onions, chopped
3 tablespoons canned green peppercorns,
    in their liquid
¾ cup dry white wine
1 tablespoon lemon juice
1 teaspoon Dijon mustard
⅓ cup heavy cream
Salt and ground black pepper

Bone and skin the chicken breasts and cut into thin scallops. Melt half the butter in the wok and sauté the chicken until cooked through (about 3½ minutes); then remove and keep warm.

Add the onions to the wok and cook until softened; then set aside with the chicken.

Add the peppercorns in their liquid and the wine to the wok and bring to a boil. Simmer for about 10 minutes until the wine is well reduced. Add the remaining butter, the lemon juice and mustard, and mix well. Boil gently for 1 to 2 minutes, then stir in the cream and add salt and pepper to taste. Return the chicken and onions to warm through in the sauce, then serve on a bed of white rice.

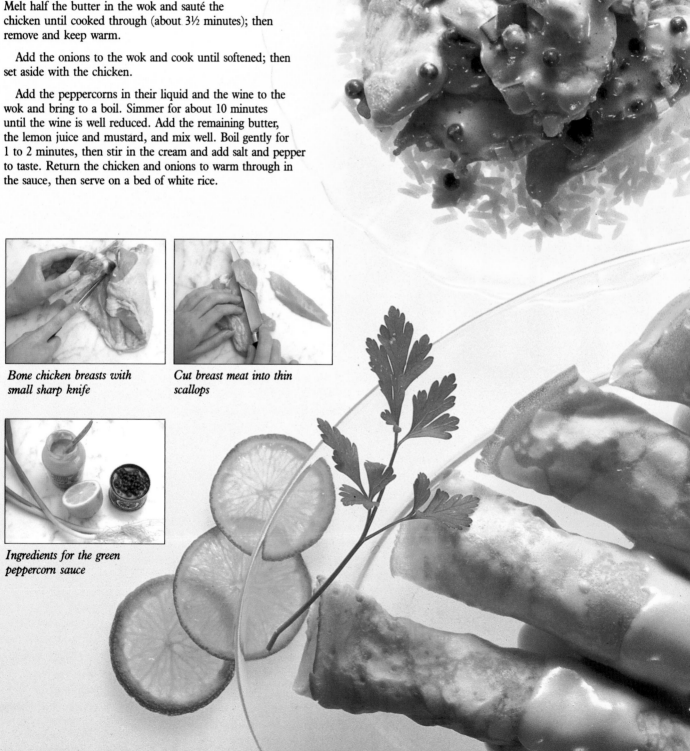

Bone chicken breasts with
small sharp knife

Cut breast meat into thin
scallops

Ingredients for the green
peppercorn sauce

Turkey and Crab Fricassee in Crêpes

SERVES 4 AS A MAIN COURSE, 8 AS AN APPETIZER

Very much a dish for special occasions, these crêpes filled with a rich creamy mixture of turkey and crab can be served as an appetizer or a main course.

Crêpes
1¼ cups flour
¾ teaspoon salt
Pinch of pepper
2 teaspoons cooking oil or melted butter
1 egg, beaten
1¾ cups milk

Filling
½ pound cooked turkey breast
⅔ cup fresh or canned crab meat
1 large spring onion
1 tablespoon parsley, chopped
1 tablespoon butter
½ chicken bouillon cube, crumbled
Salt and pepper
3½ tablespoons light dry white wine
1 cup light cream or half-and-half
1½ teaspoons cornstarch

Sauce
½ chicken bouillon cube, crumbled
½ cup dry white wine
1 bay leaf
⅓ teaspoon salt
⅓ cup butter
2 teaspoons flour
½ cup light cream
2 egg yolks, beaten

Sift the flour, salt and pepper into a mixing bowl; add the oil or butter and the egg, and mix in lightly. Then beat in the milk until the batter is the consistency of cream. Set aside for at least 30 minutes.

Shred the turkey. Drain the crab meat and flake it. Finely chop the onion. Sauté the turkey, crab meat, onion and parsley in the butter for 1 minute. Add the chicken bouillon cube, salt and pepper and the wine, and sauté, stirring, until the mixture is reduced by half.

Mix the cornstarch into the cream and then pour into the wok. Simmer, stirring, until thick; then remove from the heat and keep warm.

To make the sauce, place the chicken bouillon cube, wine, bay leaf and salt in a small saucepan; bring to a boil, then simmer until reduced by half. In another saucepan, melt 1 tablespoon of butter, then add the flour and cook until golden (about 1½ minutes). Strain in the reduced bouillon and wine, mix well and boil gently for 2 minutes. Add the cream and beat on moderate heat until thick and smooth; then add the remaining butter and heat until it begins to melt. Remove from the heat, whisk in the beaten egg yolks and continue to whisk the sauce until thick and smooth. Set aside.

Rinse out the wok and dry it thoroughly. Rub with an oiled cloth, then place over moderate heat. Pour in a large spoonful of the batter and tilt the wok so that the batter spreads thinly across the base. Cook until lightly browned on the underside and beginning to bubble, then turn and cook the other side. Remove and keep warm while the remaining crêpes are cooked. When done, fill the crêpes with the filling and top with a spoonful of the sauce. Serve at once.

Add milk to batter and beat until smooth

Sauté turkey, crab meat, onion and parsley in butter

Cook large spoonfuls of batter in wok for crêpes

Fill crêpes with turkey mixture and roll up

Salmon and Peppers in Soy Sauce

SERVES 6

1 pound skinned salmon steaks
5 tablespoons light soy sauce
3 tablespoons sweet sherry or Japanese mirin (sweet rice wine)
1¼ tablespoons sugar
1 large green pepper
3 tablespoons cooking oil

Cut the salmon into 18 cubes and place in a dish. Mix the soy sauce, sherry or mirin and sugar together until the sugar has dissolved. Pour over the fish and marinate for 10 minutes, turning occasionally.

Cut the pepper into squares, discarding the seed pod and cutting away the inner white ribs.

Heat the cooking oil in the wok. Drain the fish (reserving the marinade) and sauté with the peppers for about 2 minutes. Pour in the remaining marinade, cover the pan and simmer gently for 3 minutes more. Serve hot with white rice.

To serve as an appetizer or snack, thread the fish and peppers alternately on short bamboo skewers and cook in the same way.

Trout with Almonds

SERVES 4

4 fresh trout
½ cup butter
⅓ cup flour
Salt and black pepper
⅓ cup flaked almonds
3 tablespoons lemon juice
2 tablespoons parsley, chopped

Clean the trout and wash thoroughly. Wipe dry, then stand them on a board, opening downwards. Run a rolling pin firmly from tail to head to loosen the bones. Cut through the backbone at each end with a pair of kitchen scissors and carefully pull away the bone. It should lift out in one piece, but check for any stray bones.

Heat half the butter gently in the wok. Season the flour with salt and pepper and use to lightly coat the fish. Fry the trout, two at a time, in the butter for about 2 minutes on each side, until golden and just cooked through. Do not overcook or they will become tough. Lift onto a serving plate and keep warm.

Remove skin and cut fish into 18 pieces

Sauté marinated fish and peppers in oil in wok

Stir-fried Seafood with Vegetables

SERVES 4

When all trout are cooked, add the remaining butter to the wok and cook the almonds until just golden; then add the lemon juice and parsley and cook briefly. Pour over the fish and serve at once.

¼ pound uncooked shrimp, peeled
¼ pound fresh scallops
¼ pound boneless chicken
2 teaspoons ginger wine or dry sherry
Pinch of cornstarch
1 medium carrot
½ stick celery
½ cup Chinese cabbage (*bok choy*)
6 dried Chinese mushrooms, soaked
2 tablespoons canned sliced bamboo shoots, drained
1 slice fresh gingerroot, shredded
Salt
3 tablespoons cooking oil

Sauce
½ cup chicken stock
1 teaspoon light soy sauce
1 teaspoon dry sherry
½ teaspoon salt
¼ teaspoon sugar
Pinch of white pepper
1½ teaspoons cornstarch

Run a rolling pin firmly from tail to head of fish to loosen the bones

Cut through backbone and carefully remove it in one piece

Devein shrimp and cut each into 2-3 pieces

Sprinkle chicken and seafood with ginger wine

Stir-fry the prepared vegetables in oil in wok

Wash, dry and devein the shrimp and cut into 2–3 pieces. Slice the scallops in halves, horizontally. Very thinly slice the chicken, then cut into small squares. Place the scallops and shrimp on one side of a shallow dish and the chicken on the other. Sprinkle with the ginger wine, salt and cornstarch and leave for 10 minutes.

Peel and thinly slice the carrot. Slice the celery and cabbage. Drain the mushrooms and remove the stems. Mix the sauce ingredients in a small bowl and set aside.

Heat the wok and add the cooking oil. Stir-fry the shrimp and scallops together until they whiten and firm up (about 1½ minutes); remove to a plate. Stir-fry the chicken pieces until white, then set aside with the seafood. Add the vegetables and ginger to the wok, with a little more oil if needed, and stir-fry for about 3 minutes. Pour in the sauce and bring to a boil. Simmer briefly, then return the seafood and chicken to the wok and heat through. Serve hot.

Masala Shrimp

SERVES 4 AS A MAIN COURSE, 6 AS AN APPETIZER

This tasty recipe for shrimp was discovered in a tiny fashionable restaurant in Goa. It takes its name from the fragrant Indian curry powder, Garam Masala.

12 large uncooked shrimp, in the shell (approx. 1½ pounds)
1 teaspoon clove garlic, crushed
1 tablespoon parsley, finely chopped
1 tablespoon Garam Masala, or mild curry powder
½ teaspoon salt
2 tablespoons butter
2 tablespoons cooking oil
½ cup heavy cream
Salt and black pepper

Peel the shrimp, leaving the tails intact. Slit each one open down the center backs and remove the vein. Mix the garlic, parsley, Garam Masala and salt together, and press a portion of this into the opening of each shrimp.

Heat the butter and oil together in the wok and sauté the shrimp, turning several times, until cooked through (about 6 minutes). Transfer to a serving plate.

Pour the cream into the wok and bring to a rapid boil, stirring to incorporate any spices and herbs remaining in the pan. Add salt and pepper to taste, and spoon over the shrimp. Serve at once with saffron rice.

Peel shrimp, leaving the tail intact

Press seasoning into opening of each shrimp

Sauté shrimp, turning, until cooked

Pipérade

SERVES 4–6

A nourishing and tasty egg and vegetable dish from the Basque Provinces which serves six as an appetizer or four as a main course. Traditionally, onion is not included in a Pipérade, but you may prefer to add a small, finely chopped onion for extra flavor.

3 green peppers
3 tablespoons good olive oil
1 pound ripe tomatoes
2 thick slices of cured or smoked ham, diced
Salt and black pepper
5 eggs, beaten

Cut the peppers into strips after removing the stems, seed pods and inner ribs. Sauté in the oil for 5 minutes.

Drop the tomatoes into boiling water and remove at the count of eight. Peel, then chop finely. Add to the peppers and cook until the vegetables are tender. Halfway through this cooking, add the ham and salt and pepper to taste. Just before serving, add the eggs, stir in lightly and increase the heat. Cook, stirring, until the egg is just set.

Cut raw, smoked ham into dice

Add eggs to stir-fried vegetables

Deep-frying

The wok has all the features required of a domestic deep-fryer. Its wide top allows plenty of room for the expansion of oil. Its large capacity means that the food for a meal can be fried in one batch, eliminating the problem of keeping some warm and still crisp while the remainder is being cooked.

Its depth means that the oil can be sufficiently deep—a must for perfect deep-frying—and its sloped sides keep the bulk of the oil in the center directly above the heat source. It is inexpensive to purchase and inexpensive to use, as its unique shape requires a minimum of oil to achieve sufficient depth for use. This is particularly the case when deep-frying only a few items.

Deep-frying continues to be the one really dangerous activity in the kitchen, with countless seriously injured victims treated every year. Deep-frying should always be undertaken with great care. But with a wok, at least one of the major hazards is greatly diminished. The oil heats in the center of the wok and outward and upward toward the rim. When food is added, particularly in the case of French Fries—the most common recorded cause of kitchen fires—which have a high water content, there will be considerable active bubbling of the oil as it burns off the water. These burning hot bubbles spread toward the rim, and there are subjected to cooler air and cooler metal which help prevent an overflow. Woks are not foolproof, but they are decidedly safer than a straight-sided pan in this respect.

Mastering the art of deep-frying means that a wide variety of interesting new dishes can be included in your family meals. Food that is fried properly should be crisp and dry on the surface, light and moist inside. There shouldn't be an excessive absorption of the cooking fat or oil, and the result shouldn't be heavy, stodgy food high in calories.

Deep-frying (continued)

A fairly large wok is the best. It need not be a good-quality one, although a thick base does give best results. The accessories needed for deep-frying are a wire or metal ladle/skimmer or slotted (perforated) spoon; a draining rack or plentiful supply of paper towels; and a pair of long-handled tongs or wooden chopsticks to retrieve individual items from the oil. A small French Fry basket, which will fit down into the center of the oil, would be useful for cooking small items, including herbs such as parsley. Some woks come equipped with a wire draining rack, which fits on the inner rim of the wok. This can be useful, but is not essential.

Always have the wok lid on hand when deep-frying. If the oil should ignite, the flames will be quickly snuffed out when the wok is covered with its lid.

The temperature of deep oil is crucial for successful frying. Temperatures begin at about 350°F and range up to 425°F for certain foods that require just a quick hot fry. Higher temperatures would burn the oil; lower temperatures would mean that the coating of the food would become oil-saturated and damp.

While a thermometer to gauge the oil temperature would be useful, there is a simple test that can be applied prior to cooking, using day-old bread cut into 1-inch cubes. To turn the bread a crisp golden-brown, it will require:

90 seconds when oil is at 350°F/moderate;
60 seconds when oil is at 375°F/moderately hot;
30 seconds when oil is at 425°F/hot.

This simple scale can be used for all deep-frying.

The best cooking mediums to use for deep-frying are a good-quality cooking (vegetable) oil, peanut oil, lard (pork fat), ghee (clarified butter) or olive oil. Cooking (vegetable) oil is the obvious choice for the majority of dishes, as it is relatively inexpensive, has little of its own flavor to impart to the food and no offensive odors. Olive oil is unsuitable for sweets. Lard and ghee are rich and are best for sweet foods. Butter cannot be used for deep-frying, as it would burn long before it reached the required temperature.

There should be at least 3 inches of oil in the center of the pan and about 3 inches space allowed above the oil surface for bubbling up and the bulk of the ingredients.

Once the correct temperature has been reached, it is important to retain this throughout the cooking. The temperature will lower slightly at each addition of food, but will then begin to build up again as the food warms.

Avoid attempting to cook too many pieces of food at any one time. This will cause the temperature of the oil to drop dramatically, the food will absorb too much oil, and will stew rather than fry crisply. At any one time, cook only as much as will allow the oil to continue to bubble briskly. It may be necessary to slightly reduce the cooking temperature after the initial 1 or 2 minutes of frying, to prevent a temperature increase that would cause the food to cook too quickly on the outside, making it dark before the inside is cooked through. To achieve crispness, it is often necessary to fry foods a second time. Cook the items once until just cooked through and a light golden color, then remove and drain well. Allow to cool slightly and, in the meantime, reheat the oil to a slightly higher temperature than before. Return the food and fry for about 1 minute.

Frying oils and fats need not be discarded after each use. If correctly cared for and never burnt, they can be reused many times. After each use, the oil or fat should be strained from the wok through a fine filter or wire strainer. Ideal is the French *chinois*, a conical strainer of fine mesh that is fitted with a filter similar to a coffee filter. A piece of clean muslin or cheesecloth can serve the same purpose.

An easy method for purifying oil is to peel and slice a potato and add the pieces after each use. As the oil or fat cools, the potato is cooked and draws onto itself many of the fine particles that discolor the oil.

When frying oil has become very darkened and discolored, it is time to discard it and start again. But this can be postponed indefinitely by adding a little new oil at each use. If frying fat smokes excessively when heated, it should be discarded.

Should oil or fat become overheated, the temperature can be reduced quickly to avoid burning by adding a quantity of cold oil or a large spoonful of cold fat and, of course, removing from the heat. Never add water to oil or fat to cool it. In fact, avoid even small splashes of water getting into hot oil or fat because they can splutter dangerously. Ensure that all utensils are thoroughly dried before using in the oil.

Foods should be dried on paper towels before frying, both to avoid spluttering and to ensure that the surface will cook crisp and dry.

There are two main types of foods that are deep-fried: those that are coated, e.g. battered, breaded, dusted with flour, dipped in beaten egg white; and those that are uncoated, such as whole poultry, whole fish, pastries and potatoes.

The following scale gives temperature requirements and approximate cooking times for various fried foods.

Potatoes	French Fries	350°F for 4–5 minutes, then 425°F for 2 minutes
	Potato Chips	425°F for 2 minutes
	Shoestring Potatoes	350°F for 3 minutes, then 425°F for 1 minute
Poultry	Cuts/portions	375°F for 7–8 minutes
	Scallops/croquettes	375°F for 3 minutes
Fish	Fillets	375°F for 4 minutes
	Fingers	375°F for 2–3 minutes
Scallops	Whole, coated	190°C (375°F) for 2–3 minutes
Shrimp	Whole, coated	375°F for 2–3 minutes
Fritters		350°F for 3 minutes

Iranian Meatballs

MAKES 24

A variety of aromatic spices and fresh herbs combine to make these tempting meatballs from the Middle East.

1 pound ground beef
2 slices white bread, crusts removed
1 medium onion, grated
2 cloves garlic, crushed
3 tablespoons chopped fresh herbs (including parsley and mint)
½ teaspoon ground allspice
1½ teaspoons ground coriander
½ teaspoon ground cumin
Pinch of powdered cinnamon
1 teaspoon salt
¼ teaspoon ground black pepper
2 eggs
1¼ cups dry bread crumbs

Place the meat in a food processor or meat grinder and work until smooth and pasty. Remove to a mixing bowl. Cut the bread into cubes, place in the processor and work to crumbs, then mix with the meat. Add the onion, herbs, spices, salt and pepper, plus one of the eggs. Mix thoroughly, then work to a smooth paste and form into 24 balls.

Beat the remaining egg. Dip the meatballs into the egg and coat with the crumbs. Chill for 45 minutes.

Heat deep oil to moderately hot. Deep-fry the meatballs in several batches until golden brown and cooked through. Drain and serve hot with a garnish of orange slices and sprigs of mint.

Use wet hands to roll meatballs

Coat meatballs with egg and bread crumbs

Camembert Stuffed with Shrimp

SERVES 4

1 Camembert cheese
¼ cup small shrimp, cooked and peeled
1 egg, beaten
3 tablespoons dry bread crumbs
2¼ tablespoons white sesame seeds
2½ cups oil

Cut the Camembert into four wedges. Make a slit in the center of each and insert several small shrimp. Close up and pinch the edges together to reshape.

Dip into the beaten egg and coat lightly with the crumbs, then dip into the egg again and coat with sesame seeds. Place on a tray and refrigerate for 1 hour.

Heat oil in the wok to moderately hot. Put in the Camembert and deep-fry until golden brown. Drain and serve at once on folded paper napkins.

Insert shrimp in wedges of camembert

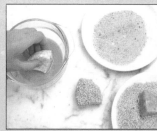
Coat camembert in egg and crumbs, then egg and sesame

Shrimp Toast

MAKES 12

1 cup shrimp, peeled
¾ cup fresh white
    bread crumbs
1 egg white, lightly
    beaten
1½ teaspoons lemon juice
¾ teaspoon salt
1 teaspoon cornstarch
6 slices fresh white bread
1 egg, beaten
1 tablespoon white
    sesame seeds

Finely mince the shrimp and mix with the bread crumbs, egg white, lemon juice, salt and cornstarch, working to a smooth paste.

Remove the crusts from the bread and cut each slice into halves. Brush one side of each piece with beaten egg and cover with a thick layer of the shrimp paste, smoothing the edges with the back of a spoon dipped in cold water. Brush the tops with more beaten egg and sprinkle on a few of the sesame seeds.

Heat deep oil to moderately hot. Deep-fry the shrimp toasts, several at a time and fillings downwards, until golden and crisp (about 1¼ minutes). Turn and cook the other sides, then drain well on paper towels before serving. These are particularly good with drinks before dinner.

Brush bread with egg, coat with the shrimp mixture

Brush with more egg and dip in sesame seeds

Deep-fry shrimp toasts, several at a time

Scallop Puffs

MAKES 36

⅔ cup fresh scallops
½ cup canned mushrooms, drained
3 tablespoons butter
1 tablespoon onion, grated
½ clove garlic, crushed
¼ teaspoon fennel seeds, crushed
3½ tablespoons flour
¼ cup milk
½ teaspoon English mustard powder
2 teaspoons lemon juice
1 package frozen puff pastry

Finely chop the scallops and mushrooms. Sauté in the butter
with the onion, garlic and fennel seeds for about 2 minutes.
Sprinkle on the flour and continue cooking until lightly
browned.

Heat the milk with the mustard in a small saucepan. Pour
into the scallop mixture, and stir on moderate heat until thick
and smooth (about 5 minutes), stirring constantly. Remove
from the heat, add the lemon juice and leave to cool.

Roll out the pastry fairly thinly and cut into 36 rounds using
a 1¼-inch circular cutter. Then roll each pastry out individually
until very thin and almost transparent. Place a spoonful of the
filling in the center of each pastry and fold over to form
crescents. Pinch the edges together, using a little milk or
beaten egg to stick them down, if needed.

Heat deep oil to moderately hot and fry the puffs, several at
a time, until golden and well expanded. Drain well on paper
towels and serve hot.

Sprinkle flour onto sautéed scallop mixture

Roll pastry rounds out until almost transparent

Place filling on each round and form a crescent

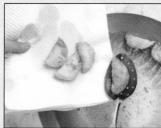
Fry puffs in hot oil and drain on paper towels

Crisp and Spicy Squid

SERVES 4

1 pound fresh small squid
1 teaspoon clove garlic, crushed
¾ teaspoon freshly ground black pepper
2 egg whites, lightly beaten
⅓ cup flour
1¼ teaspoons salt
¾ teaspoon cayenne pepper
1 cup olive oil
2 cups cooking oil
Lemon juice

Clean the squid under running cold water, removing heads, stomach sacs, skin and fins. Rinse well, then cut the tubular bodies into thin rings. Place in a dish, add the garlic and pepper, and mix thoroughly. Set aside at room temperature for 1 hour.

Drain the squid, dry on paper towels, then dip into the egg whites. Coat with the flour which has been seasoned with the salt and cayenne pepper.

Heat the olive and cooking oil together in the wok until smoking hot. Reduce heat slightly. Deep-fry the squid in two or three batches until crisp and golden. Drain well and serve hot dressed with lemon juice.

Clean squid under running cold water

Use a cube of bread to test temperature of oil

Stuffed Crab Claws

MAKES 12

12 crab claws, with meat intact
½ pound crab meat
½ pound peeled shrimp
1⅓ cups fresh white bread crumbs
2 small eggs, beaten
1 teaspoon salt
¼ teaspoon freshly ground black pepper
2 teaspoons lemon juice
⅓ teaspoon English mustard powder

Remove the shell from the crab claws, leaving meat attached just to the points of the claws. Place the other crab meat, shrimp, ½ cup of the bread crumbs and the remaining ingredients in a food processor or blender and work to a smooth paste. Form into 12 balls and push a finger through the center of each. Insert the claw meat into the cavity, leaving the pincer protruding. Squeeze the mixture firmly onto the crab claw. You may find it easier to do this if you wet your hands with cold water first. Coat each crab claw with the remaining bread crumbs.

Heat deep oil to moderately hot. Deep-fry the crab claws, several at a time, until cooked through and golden-brown on the surface (about 2½ minutes). Drain well and serve hot with a chili or soy sauce dip.

Some crab claws have shell partly removed as shown

Form mixture into balls and insert the crab claw

Chicken Wings with Plum Sauce

SERVES 6

6 chicken wings (approx. 1 pound)
1 tablespoon Hoisin sauce (sweet bean paste)
2 teaspoons dry sherry
1 teaspoon fresh gingerroot, grated
1 clove garlic, crushed
¾ teaspoon salt
½ cup cornstarch
2 tablespoons Chinese plum sauce

Remove the wing tips and keep for soup making. Wipe the wings with paper towels and place in a dish. Add the Hoisin sauce, sherry, ginger, garlic and salt and mix thoroughly, rubbing it evenly into the wings. Leave for 30 minutes to absorb the flavorings, then drain on paper towels and coat thickly with the cornstarch.

Heat deep oil to fairly hot, then decrease the heat slightly. Put in the wings to deep-fry for about 4½ minutes, turning frequently. Remove with a slotted spoon and arrange on a serving dish. Pour on the plum sauce and serve at once.

Remove wing tip and keep for soup making

Rub Hoisin sauce mixture evenly over wings

Coat wings with cornstarch and deep-fry in hot oil

Stuffed Mini Drumsticks

MAKES 6

6 chicken wings (approx. 1 pound)★
½ teaspoon fresh gingerroot, grated
1 teaspoon spring onion, finely chopped
2 teaspoons light soy sauce
Seasoned cornstarch
1 large egg, beaten
1¼ cups fresh (soft) white bread crumbs

Filling
6 tablespoons finely ground beef or pork
1 (8-ounce) can water chestnuts, drained
1 spring onion, chopped
¼ teaspoon fresh gingerroot, grated
¼ teaspoon crushed garlic
2 teaspoons light soy sauce
½ teaspoon dark soy sauce
½ teaspoon dry sherry
½ teaspon sugar
2 teaspoons cornstarch

Sweet and Sour Sauce
1 tablespoon cooking oil
1 tablespoon fresh gingerroot, chopped
½ teaspoon crushed garlic
½ cup chicken stock
¼ cup sugar
⅓ cup white vinegar
Pinch of salt and pepper
1 tablespoon chopped Chinese mixed pickles or
    ginger preserved in syrup
2½ teaspoons cornstarch
Red food coloring (optional)

Scrape away the meat from the bones of the wings, working from the larger end, and push the meat over the smaller end of the bone to form a ball shape with a cavity in the center of the top. Place in a dish with the grated ginger, spring onion and soy sauce and leave for 20 minutes.

Place the beef or pork, water chestnuts and onion in a food processor or blender and work to a smooth paste; then add the ginger, garlic and seasonings. Stir in the cornstarch and knead the mixture until smooth and thoroughly amalgamated. Fill into the cavities of the wings and smooth the tops into ball shapes.

Coat lightly with seasoned cornstarch, then dip into the beaten egg and coat with the crumbs. Place on a dish and chill for 1 hour before frying to firm the filling and to prevent the crumbs flaking off during cooking.

Heat deep oil to fairly hot and fry the drumsticks, two or three at a time, until golden and cooked through (about 5 minutes). Drain and serve with Sweet and Sour Sauce.

To make the Sweet and Sour Sauce, mix together in a clean wok or saucepan the oil, ginger, garlic, chicken stock, sugar, vinegar, salt, pepper and pickles. Blend the cornstarch with 1 tablespoon of the liquid from the pickles or ginger and stir in. Bring to a boil and simmer for 2 to 3 minutes. A touch of red food coloring can be added. Serve hot.

★ *Use only the upper (shoulder) joint of the wings, reserving the tips and central joints for another recipe.*

Use meaty portion of chicken wings

Scrape meat away from the bones to form a ball

Fill cavity in ball of chicken with beef mixture

Dip in egg and coat with bread crumbs before frying

Spring Rolls

MAKES 18

½ **pound boneless chicken**
2 **teaspoons light soy sauce**
2 **teaspoons dry sherry**
¼ **teaspoon salt**
¼ **teaspoon sugar**
¼ **red pepper**
2 **tablespoons canned sliced bamboo shoots, drained**
1 **medium carrot, peeled**
¼ **pound fresh bean sprouts**
2 **cabbage or spinach leaves**
3 **tablespoons cooking oil**
2 **spring onions, shredded**
1 **slice fresh gingerroot, shredded**
1 **package of 8-inch frozen spring-roll wrappers**

Sauce
¾ **teaspoon salt**
1 **teaspoon sugar**
2 **teaspoons light soy sauce**
2 **teaspoons cornstarch**
1 **tablespoon cold water**

Thinly slice the chicken, then cut into narrow shreds. Place in a dish and add the soy sauce, sherry, salt and sugar; mix well and leave for 20 minutes.

Remove stem, seed pod and inner ribs from the pepper. Shred the pepper, bamboo shoots and carrot into julienne (matchstick) strips. Rinse and thoroughly drain the bean sprouts. Finely shred the cabbage or spinach leaves.

Heat the cooking oil in the wok and stir-fry the chicken until white. Remove and keep warm. Add the vegetables, onions and ginger to the wok and stir-fry until tender. Return the chicken and add the premixed sauce ingredients. Simmer, stirring, until there is no liquid in the bottom of the pan, then transfer to a plate to cool.

Thaw the spring-roll wrappers under a cloth, then separate and keep covered. To wrap, place a portion of the filling in the center of each wrapper; fold over one corner and shape the filling into a roll, fold in the two sides, then roll up tightly. Dip the end in water and stick down. If water is not effective in sticking down the ends, make a paste by boiling 1 tablespoon of cornstarch with about ⅓ cup of water, and brush this on.

Heat oil for deep-frying in a clean wok and fry several rolls at a time in moderately hot oil, for about 3 minutes. Drain on paper towels and keep warm while the remainder are being cooked. Serve hot with Sweet and Sour Sauce (see page 41) or dips of light soy and chili sauces.

Place filling on spring-roll wrapper and fold

Roll up and dip end in cold water to seal

Spring rolls can be made in two sizes

Pork Wontons

MAKES 48

1 pound fatty pork
2 tablespoons fresh bean sprouts
1 (8-ounce) can water chestnuts, drained
2 spring onions, chopped
1 tablespoon parsley, finely chopped
½ teaspoon fresh gingerroot, grated
1½ teaspoons salt
¼ teaspoon pepper
2 teaspoons sugar
1 tablespoon light soy sauce
2 teaspoons cornstarch
48 frozen or fresh wonton wrappers

Cut the pork into small cubes and place in a food processor or blender; grind to a smooth paste. Finely chop the bean sprouts and chestnuts, and add to the pork with the remaining ingredients—excluding the wrappers, of course. Mix thoroughly, kneading until fairly smooth. Wrap in a piece of plastic wrap and chill for 1 hour.

Thaw and separate the wonton wrappers and cover with a cloth. To fill, place a teaspoonful of the mixture in the center of a wrapper and pinch the edges together encasing the filling. The edges must be brushed with a little water in order to seal.

Wontons can be made in a variety of shapes. The *Purse* has its edges all drawn up together into a point at the center of the top. The *Goldfish* is formed by folding three edges one over the other to give a smooth ball shape on top, and the remaining corner is fluted out and down to form the tail. To make a *Swimming Fish*, pull three corners up and over the filling in the center, and the remaining corner is fluted upwards and outwards in a tail shape. To make the *Bon Bon*, the wrapper is rolled around the filling and the ends are twisted to resemble a wrapped candy.

Heat oil for deep-frying until fairly hot. Fry about eight at a time, until golden (about 2½ minutes). Drain and serve hot on a bed of Fried Chinese Cabbage (see page 46).

Purse-shaped and goldfish wontons

Swimming fish and bon bon wontons

Vegetable Curry Triangles
Samosas

MAKES 36

2 medium potatoes
¼ pound peas
1 medium onion
¼ pound cauliflower, chopped
1 tablespoon butter
2 teaspoons Garam Masala, or hot curry powder
1 tablespoon parsley, chopped
1 teaspoon chopped fresh mint, or a pinch of
    dried mint
2 teaspoons lemon juice
1 teaspoon salt
1 package of 10-inch frozen spring-roll wrappers

Boil the potatoes in their jackets in lightly salted water, then peel and cut into dice. Boil the peas until tender, then drain. Peel and finely chop the onion.

Sauté the onion and cauliflower in the butter until tender and lightly browned. Add the potatoes and peas and sauté briefly. Then add the spices, herbs, lemon juice and salt, and mix well. Transfer to a plate and leave to cool.

Thaw the spring-roll wrappers under a cloth, then separate and keep covered. When ready to use, cut into strips about 1¾ inches wide.

To fill, turn over one end to form a triangular pouch and fill with about 2 teaspoons of the filling. Wrap up the pastries, keeping to the triangular shape and enclosing the filling. Brush the ends with cold water and press into place.

Heat deep oil to hot. Deep-fry the pastries, several at a time, until golden. Lift out with a slotted spoon and drain well before serving hot. Tomato sauce spiked with chili makes a tasty accompaniment.

Separate the thawed spring-roll wrappers

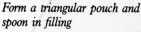

Form a triangular pouch and spoon in filling

Fold up pastries

Curry Puffs Taj Mahal

MAKES 18

Pastry
¾ cup flour
¼ teaspoon salt
1 large egg, beaten
1 tablespoon butter or margarine, softened
Lukewarm water

Filling
½ pound lean ground beef
3 tablespoons butter
¼ cup cooked peas
1 medium onion, chopped
2 cloves garlic, crushed
½ teaspoon fresh gingerroot, grated
2½ teaspoons hot curry powder
¼ to ½ teaspoon chili powder
¾ teaspoon salt
Pinch of black pepper
1 tablespoon fresh mint or parsley, chopped
1 tablespoon lemon juice

Sift the flour and salt into a mixing bowl and make a well in the center. Add the egg and the softened butter or margarine, and work in lightly. Add just enough water to make a reasonably firm dough. Lift the dough onto a lightly floured board and knead gently until smooth. Wrap in plastic wrap and chill until needed.

Sauté the beef in butter until lightly browned. Stir it continuously to separate the pieces. Add the peas and sauté lightly; then add the onion, garlic and ginger and continue to cook for 5 to 6 minutes. If the mixture begins to stick to the bottom of the pan, splash in a very little cold water from time to time. Add the curry and chili powders and the salt and pepper and cook for 1 to 2 minutes more. Remove from the heat and stir in the chopped herbs and lemon juice. Spread on a plate to cool.

Knead the dough again lightly, then roll out into a large, thin sheet; trim the sides straight and cut into eighteen 3-inch squares. Divide the filling among the pastries. Fold each in half to give triangular shapes. The edges should be brushed with milk to help them stick. Use the prongs of a fork to indent a pattern around the edges.

Fold the two extreme points over to meet and slightly overlap in the center front, and use a little more egg or milk to stick it down. The finished pastry should resemble an open envelope.

Heat deep oil to moderately hot. Deep-fry the pastries, several at a time, until golden. Lift out with a slotted spoon and drain well. Serve hot with sweet chutney, mint sauce or tomato sauce.

Knead pastry gently until smooth

Place filling in center of pastry square; fold over

Press edge with fork to seal and decorate

Fold points in to form an envelope

Fried Chinese Cabbage

This crisply fried green vegetable can be served as a side dish or used as a delicious edible garnish with fried appetizers such as Shrimp Toast (page 37) or Pork Wontons (page 43).

12 large leaves of Chinese cabbage (*bok choy*)
¾ teaspoon sugar
1 teaspoon sesame oil
2 teaspoons white sesame seeds

Finely shred the *bok choy* leaves, discarding any stems, and place them in a frying basket. Heat deep oil to moderately hot and insert the basket. Fry until the *bok choy* is bright green and rustles when the basket is shaken over the oil. Drain well on paper towels and place in a serving dish. Combine the remaining ingredients, pour over the *bok choy* and mix thoroughly.

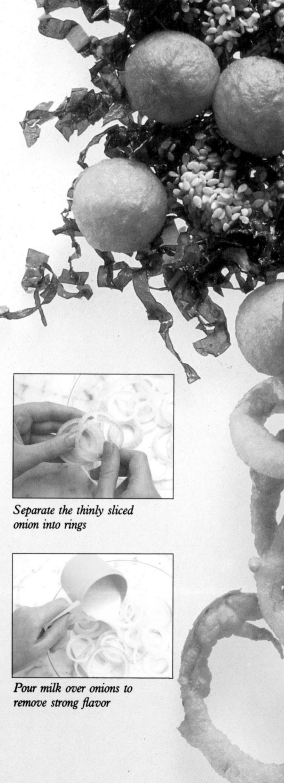

Finely shred the leaves of the bok choy

Plunge the bok choy into oil until bright green

Onion Rings

SERVES 4

2 medium onions
1 cup milk
1 cup flour
1 egg, beaten
¼ teaspoon salt

Peel the onions and slice fairly thinly. Separate into rings and place in a dish. Pour on the milk and leave for 1 hour. The milk will draw off some of the strong flavor from the onion.

Drain the onions thoroughly, reserving the milk. Mix the milk with the flour, egg and salt, beating to a smooth batter.

Heat deep oil in the wok. Dip the onion rings one by one into the batter and place in the oil. Cook only eight to ten at a time, turning when the underside has become golden. Drain thoroughly. Keep warm while the remainder are cooked. These can be made a short time in advance and quickly refried in very hot oil just before serving to ensure crispness.

Separate the thinly sliced onion into rings

Pour milk over onions to remove strong flavor

Pommes Noisette

SERVES 6

1½ pounds large potatoes
Seasoned flour

Peel and wash the potatoes and use a melon scoop to cut out balls with a diameter of about ¾ inch. Parboil in lightly salted water, then drain thoroughly and leave to cool and dry. Coat lightly with the seasoned flour.

Heat deep oil to moderately hot. Deep-fry the potato balls until golden (about 5 minutes). Remove and leave to cool slightly while the oil reheats. Return the potatoes to the oil and fry for 1 to 1½ minutes more, until very crisp and golden on the surface. Drain on paper towels, sprinkle with salt and serve.

Cut potatoes into balls with melon baller

Dry parboiled potatoes thoroughly before frying

Crisp Zucchini or Eggplant Slices

SERVES 4

This is a delicious way to use up older vegetables.

1 large eggplant, or 1 or 2 long, thin zucchini
1 cup flour
Salt and pepper
3 tablespoons Parmesan cheese, grated

Thinly slice the vegetables without peeling and spread on a board or tray. Sprinkle generously with salt and leave for 1 hour. The salt will draw off the bitter juices.

Rinse the vegetables thoroughly, then dry on a cloth. Season the flour with salt and pepper and coat the vegetables.

Heat deep oil to fairly hot. Deep-fry the vegetables in two or three batches until crisp and golden. Drain and transfer to a serving dish, sprinkle on the cheese and serve at once.

Thinly slice zucchini or eggplant   Sprinkle salt on zucchini to remove bitter juices

Chicken Kebabs

MAKES 12

This simplified version of Indonesian Satay can be served as an appetizer or main course. Cook it without the chili powder as a treat for a children's party.

¾ pound boneless chicken breasts
2 teaspoons lemon juice
1 teaspoon mild curry powder
Pinch of chili powder or cayenne pepper
¼ teaspoon salt

Batter
1 cup flour
1 cup water
½ teaspoon salt
1 teaspoon baking powder
½ teaspoon mild curry powder
½ cup dry bread crumbs

Skin the chicken breasts and rub with a mixture of the lemon juice, curry, chili powder (or cayenne) and the salt. Place on a covered plate and set aside at room temperature for 10 minutes to absorb the flavors.

Cut the chicken meat into 12 strips and thread each strip onto a bamboo or metal skewer. Mix the batter ingredients, except bread crumbs, together in a bowl. Spread the crumbs on a plate.

Heat deep oil to moderately hot in the wok. Dip the chicken into the batter, then coat with crumbs. Place in the deep oil to fry for about 2½ minutes, or until cooked through and golden brown on the surface. Serve hot with wedges of lemon and a sweet chutney.

Rub chicken meat with juice and curry powder

Cut chicken into strips and thread on skewers

Deep-fry the battered and breaded kebabs

Chicken Supreme

SERVES 4 AS A MAIN COURSE, 8 AS AN APPETIZER

1 (2½-pound) roasting chicken
½ pound uncooked shrimp, peeled
2 spring onions
1 (8-ounce) can water chestnuts, drained
1 slice fresh gingerroot
2 teaspoons ginger wine or dry sherry
¾ teaspoon salt
Cornstarch

Sauce A
½ cup chicken stock
2 teaspoons oyster sauce
½ teaspoon light soy sauce
½ teaspoon sugar
1 tablespoon cooking oil
¾ teaspoon cornstarch

Sauce B
½ cup bottled Chinese plum sauce
2 teaspoons tomato sauce

Clean the chicken, cut in half and trim away the backbone. Use a short, narrow-bladed knife to carefully debone the chicken, leaving just the first section of the wing bone in position. Cut off the two lower joints of the wings, and the drumsticks and thighs, and reserve for another recipe. Set the chicken aside.

Devein the shrimp and place in a food processor or blender with the trimmed onions, water chestnuts, ginger, wine or sherry and salt. Work to a smooth paste.

Dust the meaty side of the chicken halves with cornstarch, then coat each with the shrimp paste. Coat with more cornstarch, then cover with a piece of plastic wrap and chill for at least 1 hour, to help hold the filling on the chicken during cooking.

When ready to cook, heat deep oil to moderately hot. Coat the chicken again with cornstarch, brushing off the excess. Place in the oil to fry gently for about 15 minutes. Turn the chicken using tongs to avoid breaking the skin. Drain well.

Serve with Sauce A or Sauce B, depending on which would best suit other dishes on the menu. Bring Sauce A ingredients to a boil in a small saucepan and simmer, stirring, until thickened. Heat Sauce B just to boiling point. The sauce may be poured over the chicken or served separately.

Carefully remove bones from the half chicken

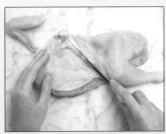

Cut off wings, thigh and drumstick

Spread with shrimp mixture; coat with cornstarch

Fisherman's Basket

SERVES 6

3 fish fillets
¼ pound scallops
12 uncooked shrimp, in the shell
12 fresh oysters
1 large bunch parsley
Cornstarch
2 lemons

Egg White Batter
1 cup flour
½ cup cornstarch
1 teaspoon salt
2 teaspoons baking powder
1 cup water
2 large egg whites

Tartar Sauce
1 cup thick mayonnaise
1 teaspoon dry mustard
½ teaspoon dried tarragon
2 teaspoons chopped chives
2 teaspoons capers, chopped
2 teaspoons gherkins, chopped
1 teaspoon anchovy, mashed (optional)
Salt and pepper

Prepare the seafood and parsley

Fold whipped egg whites into the batter

Plunge parsley into hot oil for 20 seconds

Cut each fish fillet into four pieces. Remove the roe from the scallops, if necessary. Peel the shrimp, leaving the tails intact; devein and rinse in cold water. Remove oysters from the shell and rinse in lightly salted water. Wash the parsley, shake out excess water, then wrap in a paper towel until needed.

To make the egg white batter, sift the flour, cornstarch, salt and baking powder into a mixing bowl and add the water. Beat until smooth, then set aside for about 15 minutes. Add a very little more water if the mixture seems too thick; it should be the consistency of thick cream.

Whip the egg whites to soft peaks and fold carefully into the batter. Once the eggs have been incorporated, the batter should be used at once.

Heat deep oil to moderate. Pat the seafood pieces dry with paper towels and coat lightly with cornstarch, shaking off excess. Dip into the batter and deep-fry, several pieces at a time, until cooked through, crisp and golden. Drain on paper towels. When all are cooked, arrange in small baskets lined with paper napkins or on a pretty serving dish.

Place the parsley in a frying basket and plunge into the oil to cook for about 20 seconds until bright green and crisp. Drain well and arrange around the seafood, adding several lemon wedges to each basket. Serve hot with Tartar Sauce.

To make the Tartar Sauce, mix the ingredients together and allow to stand for about 3 hours before serving. Store in an airtight jar in the refrigerator.

Shrimp in Wine and Chili Sauce

SERVES 2

12 shrimp cutlets*
5 cloves garlic, sliced
3 slices gingerroot, shredded
1 large red chili, sliced
2 spring onions, sliced
3 tablespoons oil
2 egg whites
½ cup cornstarch

Sauce
2 teaspoons light
  soy sauce
2 teaspoons sugar
3½ tablespoons dry sherry
3½ tablespoons chicken
  stock
Small pinch of salt
1 teaspoon cornstarch

Mix sauce ingredients

Flour shrimp, dip in batter then in cornstarch

Deep-fry shrimp until crisp, then drain

Wash the shrimp and dry thoroughly; set aside. Mix the sauce ingredients.

Sauté the garlic, ginger, chili and onions in about 2 tablespoons of cooking oil for 1 minute. Add the premixed sauce ingredients and bring to a boil. Stir on moderate heat for 2 minutes, then set aside.

Beat the egg whites to soft peaks, then fold in half of the cornstarch. Dust the shrimp lightly with the remaining cornstarch, shaking off the excess.

Heat deep oil to hot. Dip the shrimp into the batter, then coat them lightly with the remaining cornstarch. Deep-fry, six at a time, until crisp. When all are done, reheat the oil and deep-fry the shrimp again for about 30 seconds. Drain well.

Pour off the oil and reheat the wok. Add the sauce and bring to a boil, then pour over the shrimp and serve.

* Peeled raw shrimp with the tail shell left on, deveined and butterflied (slit open down the center of the back and pressed open).

Honey Chili Fish

SERVES 6 AS AN APPETIZER, 4 AS A MAIN COURSE

1 pound white fish fillets (haddock/sea bass)

Beer and Wine Batter
1 cup flour
3 tablespoons cooking oil
2 tablespoons dry white wine
¾ cup beer
¾ teaspoon salt
3 egg whites

Honey and Chili Sauce
3 tablespoons clear honey
2 teaspoons chili sauce

Cut the fish into fingers of about 3½ x 1½ inches. Beat the flour, oil, wine, beer and salt together and set aside.

Heat deep oil to hot in the wok. Beat the egg whites to soft peaks and fold into the batter. Dip the fish into the batter, lower carefully into the hot oil and deep-fry until crisp and golden (about 2½ minutes), turning once. Remove on a slotted spoon and drain on paper towels. Serve immediately when all the fish is cooked, with accompanying Honey and Chili Sauce.

To make the Honey and Chili Sauce, heat the honey and chili sauce together in a small saucepan. Serve hot in a small sauceboat, or pour the sauce over the fish just before serving.

Cut fish in finger-sized pieces

Dip fish into beer batter and lower into hot oil

Sweet and Sour Shrimp

SERVES 4

¾ pound shrimp cutlets★
3 tablespoons cornstarch
½ small carrot
2-inch piece of cucumber
⅓ stick celery
¼ red pepper or chili pepper
1 spring onion
2 slices fresh gingerroot
1 canned pineapple ring, drained

Batter
½ cup flour
1 teaspoon baking powder
½ teaspoon salt
½ cup water
2 egg whites

Sweet and Sour Sauce
3 tablespoons cooking oil
½ cup sugar
½ cup white vinegar
3½ tablespoons pineapple juice
1 tablespoon cold water
2½ teaspoons cornstarch

Wipe the shrimp on paper towels and dust lightly with cornstarch. Set aside. Peel and shred the carrot and cucumber, discarding the cucumber seeds. Scrape and shred the celery. Trim away the seed pod and inner ribs of the pepper or chili and cut into long narrow shreds. Trim and shred the onion and ginger. Cut the pineapple into small cubes. Beat together the batter ingredients, except for the egg whites, and set aside.

Heat the oil for the sauce in a wok or saucepan and add the sugar. Cook on fairly high heat until the sugar is dissolved and becomes dark and syrupy. Add the remaining ingredients, well mixed, and bring to a boil. Simmer, stirring, until the sauce thickens. Add the carrot and cucumber and boil until softened. Then add the remaining vegetables to the sauce and simmer for 1 minute. Set aside.

Rinse out the wok, if used for the sauce. Heat deep oil to hot. Beat the egg whites to soft peaks and fold into the batter. Dip the shrimp into the batter, then place in the hot oil to cook until crisp, puffed and golden (about 1¾ minutes). Lift out with a slotted spoon and drain well on paper towels. Drain the wok, reheat the sauce if necessary and pour over the shrimp. Serve at once.

* *Peeled raw shrimp with the tail shell left on, deveined and butterflied (slit open down the center of the back and pressed open).*

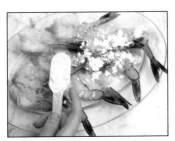
Dust shrimp cutlets lightly with cornstarch

Cut all the vegetables into shreds

Noodle Baskets

MAKES 6 INDIVIDUAL SERVING BASKETS

Chinese egg noodles can be used to make edible food containers, which look particularly attractive with seafood dishes such as Sweet and Sour Shrimp (previous recipe) or Stir-fried Seafood with Vegetables (page 29).

5 cakes of thin egg noodles

Soak the noodles in cold water until they separate. Drain very thoroughly by spreading on several layers of paper towels and covering with more paper.

Select two wire strainers, one slightly larger than the other. Dip them in deep oil and shake to remove most of the oil. Divide the noodles into six equal portions. Line the larger strainer with a portion of the noodles and press the smaller strainer inside to form noodles into a basket shape.

Heat deep oil to hot. Place the strainers in the oil, holding the two handles firmly together. Cook for about 2 minutes until the smaller basket can be lifted out without disturbing the noodles, then continue to cook until golden and crisp. Lift out, drain well, then turn upside down onto paper towels. Tap the bottom of the strainer to release the basket. Leave to drain upside down until needed.

Unused noodle baskets can be stored in an airtight container and warmed in a moderate oven when needed. To use, stand the baskets on a plate and surround with parsley or celery leaves. Fill with the prepared dish and serve.

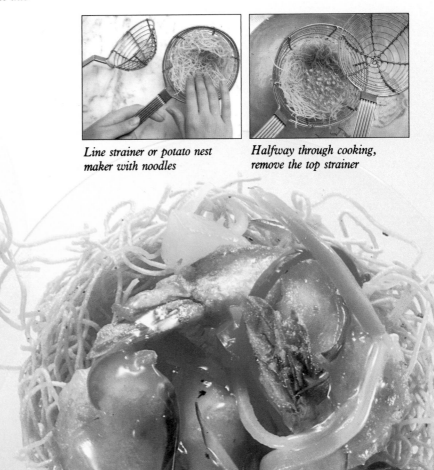
Line strainer or potato nest maker with noodles

Halfway through cooking, remove the top strainer

Almond Fingers

MAKES 36

1 cup flour
¼ teaspoon salt
1 cup water
3 tablespoons butter
2 large eggs
3 tablespoons ground almonds
1¼ cups water
1½ cups sugar
1½ teaspoons orange or rose flower water

Sift flour and salt onto a piece of greaseproof paper. In a closed wok, bring water to a boil with the butter, then quickly pour in all the flour and beat with the handle of a wooden spoon until the mixture leaves the sides of the wok and becomes a shiny smooth ball. Cook gently for about 5 minutes, stirring from time to time; then remove from the heat and transfer to a mixing bowl. Leave to partially cool, then gradually beat in the eggs and the almonds. Set aside for 10 minutes.

In a saucepan, boil the water and sugar, stirring just until the sugar dissolves. Simmer for about 10 minutes until the syrup begins to look sticky, but has not taken on any color. Remove from the heat and add the flower water. Set aside to cool.

Rinse the wok and add clean cooking oil for deep-frying. Heat to moderate. Roll out the dough and cut into small fingershapes, using wet hands to prevent sticking. Slide, several at a time, into the oil and cook for 8 to 10 minutes, until golden and puffed out. It is essential that the oil is not too hot or the pastries will cook too quickly on the outside and remain soft and sticky inside.

Remove with a slotted spoon and transfer to the cool syrup. As each batch of pastries is cooked, remove the previous batch from the syrup and place on a serving plate.

When done, the pastries can be garnished with finely chopped walnuts, toasted almonds or pistachios. Or they can be sprinkled with a mixture of cinnamon and sugar just before serving.

Add flour all at once to boiling water and butter

Stir with spoon handle until mixture forms ball

Easy Doughnuts

MAKES 12

1½ cups flour
2 teaspoons baking powder
¼ teaspoon ground cinnamon
½ cup sugar
2 teaspoons butter, melted
1 egg, beaten
Lukewarm milk

Sift the flour, baking powder and cinnamon into a mixing bowl. Add the sugar and melted butter and stir in lightly. Then add the egg and enough milk to make a soft dough. Roll out on a lightly floured board until it is about ⅓ inch thick.

Cut into rounds using a floured scone or biscuit cutter of 3 inches in diameter, then using a smaller cutter to make a hole in the center of each.

Heat clean deep oil to moderately hot. Fry the doughnuts, several at a time, until golden, turning once. When evenly browned and cooked through, remove and drain thoroughly. Cook the "holes" until golden and serve with the doughnuts.

They can be rolled in a mixture of 3 tablespoons sugar and 1½ teaspoons ground cinnamon before serving. Serve at once.

Cut dough into rounds with two cutters

Deep-fry doughnuts until golden

Toffeed Apple

SERVES 6

This is a highly regarded Chinese dessert. Not easy to get right, but worth a try!

2 large green (cooking) apples
2 tablespoons white sesame seeds
Cooking oil

Batter
1 cup flour
3 tablespoons cornstarch
1 egg, beaten
1 cup water

Toffee
1 tablespoon sesame oil
2¼ cups sugar

Peel, core and slice the apples and set aside. Mix the batter ingredients together, beating until smooth.

Heat clean deep oil to hot. Dip the apple pieces one by one into the batter and fry until crisp. Drain. When all the apple pieces have been done once, reheat the oil and fry again for 1½ minutes to crisp the batter; drain well and place on a plate near the cooking area.

Drain the wok and wipe out. Add the ingredients for the toffee and heat, stirring occasionally, until the sugar has melted and turned to a light toffee color. Add the sesame seeds and the apple pieces, and turn quickly but carefully in the toffee until evenly coated. Remove to the plate, which should be lightly oiled to prevent sticking.

Serve at once with a dish of iced water. To eat, each piece of apple should be separated from the others and dipped into the water, where the toffee will solidify.

Dip apple slices into batter

Return fried apple to hot oil briefly to crisp

Turn apple in toffee, then add sesame seeds

Shallow-frying

Shallow-frying, as an alternative to deep-frying, is usually applied to the kind of foods that require careful handling during cooking, as well as lower temperatures. Food such as uncoated fish can fall apart if allowed to bubble freely in deep oil, whereas in shallow oil they may cook gently and be turned without damage. Thin and tender scallops and cutlets coated with crumbs would become tough and chewy in deep oil, whereas shallow-frying in butter and oil will make them crisp on the surface, yet moist and flavorful inside.

A mixture of equal amounts of cooking (vegetable) oil and butter, or olive oil and butter, is the most common cooking medium for shallow-frying. The oil allows the butter to heat beyond its normal tolerance, bringing to the dish a richness of flavor that frying in oil alone would not provide. However, oil or butter alone can be used.

Shallow-frying is done in varying depths of fat, depending on the food being cooked. It can be as little as a thin spread in the bottom of the wok, or up to a depth of 2 inches in the center of the wok (using more than that would be considered deep-frying).

The fat should be heated to moderate, at which point butter will begin to foam, or oil will respond to the bread test (see the introduction to deep-frying). When the food is added to the wok, the heat can be slightly increased to counteract any cooling off caused by the cold food. When the surface is sealed on all sides, the heat can be lowered so that the food may cook gently without becoming too dark on the surface. It is essential that the wok is not crowded during shallow-frying or the food will begin to "stew" instead of frying crisply. If you are cooking too much food to fit comfortably into one wok, shallow-fry in batches, keeping the cooked food warm in the oven. Or better still, use two woks.

Tongs, wooden spoons or large metal spoons are used to turn the food, and care should be taken not to break the surface of the food—whether it be a crumb or flour coating, or its own skin—as this will allow the natural juices of the meat, for example, to escape into the cooking fat. The result will be a lowering of cooking temperature, dryness of meat and an excessive absorption of the cooking fat.

Sweet foods should be cooked in new oil, clean lard (pork fat), butter, or ghee (clarified butter); and this can then be reserved for cooking future sweet dishes. If strong flavors of spices, liqueurs, etc. have been imparted to the oil, use it again only for cooking dishes those flavors complement.

Similarly, fats used for cooking seafoods should be reserved exclusively for cooking other seafoods, as they will become strongly flavored by the seafood.

Fried foods should be well drained before serving. Paper towels are ideal for this. Take two or three sheets, place them in the bottom of a suitable dish and transfer the food from the oil to the paper to drain for a couple of minutes.

If crisply fried foods, such as crumb- or batter-coated meats or seafoods, are to be kept warm in the oven, prop the oven door slightly ajar so that steam can escape. This should help to retain their crispness.

Empanadas

MAKES 24

1 package frozen puff pastry
½ pound smoked fillet of cod or haddock
2 cups milk
3 tablespoons lard or olive oil
1 medium onion, finely chopped
1 green pepper, cored, seeded and diced
⅓ pound raw smoked ham, diced
1 tablespoon flour
¼ teaspoon cayenne pepper

Thaw the pastry and cover with a cloth until needed. Place the fish in the wok and add the milk. Cover and simmer gently until the fish is tender (about 8 minutes), then drain, reserving the milk. Skin the fish and flake it. Pick out any bones.

Heat the lard or oil in a clean wok and sauté the onion, pepper and ham for about 4 minutes. Add the flour, cayenne pepper and fish, and sauté for 1 to 2 minutes more. Then add just enough of the reserved milk to make the mixture into a thick sauce. Season with salt if needed, then remove from the wok and spread on a plate to cool.

On a lightly floured board, roll out the pastry thinly. Cut into 24 rounds, about 4 inches in diameter. Place a spoonful of the filling in the center of each pastry round. Dip a pastry brush into the remaining milk, and damp the edges of the pastry. Fold over into crescent shapes and pinch the edges together. Press the point of a fork around the edges to seal and decorate.

Shallow-fry the pastries in about 1½ inches of moderately hot cooking oil with a little olive oil added for flavor, until the pastries are golden brown and slightly puffed. Serve hot.

Place fish in wok and pour milk over it

Heat lard or oil and sauté onion, pepper and ham

Fold pastry over filling to form a crescent

Chicken "Hedgehogs"

MAKES 18

½ **pound boneless chicken**
1 **egg**
3 **tablespoons flour**
2 **teaspoons sugar**
2 **teaspoons light soy sauce**
2 **teaspoons dry sherry**
¼ **teaspoon salt**
1¼ **cups rice vermicelli**

Cut the chicken into cubes and place in a food processor with the egg, flour, sugar and other seasonings. Work to a smooth paste, then transfer to a dish. Cover with plastic wrap and chill for 20 minutes.

Form the mixture into 18 balls. Finely crush the vermicelli. Roll each ball in the noodles to coat.

Heat about 1 inch of cooking oil in the wok to moderate. Fry the "hedgehogs" about six at a time, until golden and cooked through (about 3 minutes). Drain well and serve warm with soy sauce or sweet chili sauce.

The rice vermicelli

Crush vermicelli in a plastic bag

Danish Meatballs

Frikadeller

MAKES 36

½ **pound lean veal**
½ **pound lean pork**
¼ **pound beef steak**
¼ **pound cooked ham**
1 **medium onion**
1 **teaspoon salt**
½ **teaspoon black pepper**
1 **large egg**
1 **teaspoon baking soda**
¼ **cup dry**
　bread crumbs
5 **tablespoons**
　heavy cream

Dill Mayonnaise
3 **tablespoons mayonnaise**
2 **tablespoons heavy**
　cream
¾ **teaspoon dried dillweed**
½ **teaspoon caraway seeds**

Roll meat mixture into balls and flatten tops

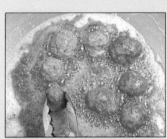

Fry about eight meatballs at a time until golden brown all over

Finely grind the meats, ham and onions, and then add the remaining ingredients, mixing thoroughly. Chill for 1 hour, then make 36 meatballs and flatten each slightly.

Heat about 1 inch cooking oil or a mixture of butter and oil in the wok to moderate. Fry the meatballs, about eight at a time, until golden brown (about 5 minutes). Drain well. Serve warm or cold with Dill Mayonnaise.

To make the Dill Mayonnaise, mix the ingredients together about 2 hours before use.

Stuffed Peppers

SERVES 4

2 large green or red peppers
½ pound finely ground pork
1 (8-ounce) can canned water chestnuts, drained
1 spring onion
½ teaspoon salt
Pinch of freshly ground black pepper
1½ teaspoons dry sherry
Cornstarch

Batter
½ cup flour
¼ cup cornstarch
1½ teaspoons baking powder
½ cup water
2 egg whites

Cut each of the peppers into quarters, lengthwise, trimming away the inner ribs and the seed stem. Place the pork in a mixing bowl. Finely chop the water chestnuts and onion, and add to the pork with the salt, pepper and sherry. Mix thoroughly, then use to fill each piece of pepper. Smooth the tops and set aside.

Mix the batter ingredients, except the egg whites, thoroughly. When ready to cook, whisk the egg whites until they stand in soft peaks, then fold into the batter.

Coat the stuffed peppers lightly with cornstarch, then dip into the batter. Shallow-fry several at a time in about 2 inches of moderately hot oil until golden, puffed out and cooked through (about 5 minutes). Drain well and serve hot.

Quarter peppers and remove ribs

Spread pork filling on pepper quarters

Dip into cornstarch, then batter

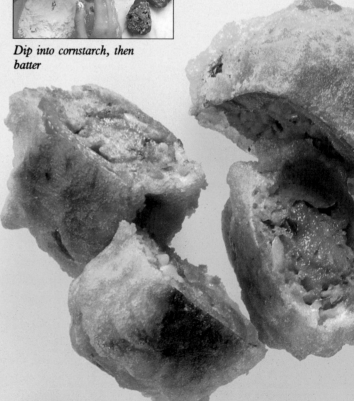

Potato Pancakes

Latkes

SERVES 4

These crisp potato pancakes are delicious as a breakfast dish, a snack or to accompany a main course. They are also worth trying as a dessert, served hot with warmed blueberries or fresh strawberries and plenty of sour cream.

1⅓ pounds raw potato, grated
¼ cup flour
2 large eggs, beaten
Salt and black pepper

Select large potatoes, peel and rinse thoroughly, and soak them in cold water for about 45 minutes. Drain and grate fairly coarsely; then squeeze out as much water as possible.

Add the flour and eggs to the potato, and season generously with salt and pepper.

Heat about ½ inch of butter and cooking oil in the wok. When foamy, add a large spoonful of the batter, pressing it into a pancake shape with the back of a spoon. Cook three or four Latkes at a time, depending on the capacity of the wok, until a deep golden brown underneath. Turn and cook the other sides until well browned. Remove and drain on paper towels.

Grate the soaked potatoes coarsely

Squeeze out as much water as possible

Sweet Corn Fritters

MAKES 24

Sweet corn fritters are a must with Chicken Maryland (page 68) but also make interesting snacks or starters, particularly before a curry dinner.

16 ounces frozen or canned sweet corn kernels
1 medium onion, grated
½ cup flour
1½ tablespoons cornstarch
2 teaspoons baking powder
¾ teaspoon chili sauce or powder
1 teaspoon salt
Pinch of freshly ground black pepper
1 egg, beaten

Thaw frozen corn or drain canned corn, then place in a food processor or blender and crush lightly. Add the onion, after draining thoroughly. Add the flour, cornstarch, baking powder, chili and seasoning; mix well, then add the egg. The mixture should be quite moist, yet thick enough to hold together in the oil. Leave for 10 to 15 minutes.

Heat about 1½ inches of oil in the wok to fairly hot. Drop in teaspoonfuls of the mixture and leave to cook until crisp and golden. Reduce the heat after the first few minutes to ensure that the fritters cook through before becoming too dark on the outside. Drain on paper towels and serve hot or warm. Hot chili sauce, soy sauce or chutney are ideal accompaniments.

Add beaten egg to sweet corn mixture

Drop spoonfuls of mixture into hot oil

Lamb Noisettes in Curry Sauce

SERVES 4

8 lamb loin chops
2 cloves garlic, crushed
1 small onion, grated

Coconut Curry Sauce
2 tablespoons cooking oil
1 large onion, grated
½ teaspoon fresh gingerroot, grated
2 cloves garlic, crushed
2 teaspoons mild curry powder
1 tomato, chopped
1¼ cups coconut milk
3 tablespoons desiccated coconut
1 teaspoon sugar
½ teaspoon salt
Pinch of freshly ground black pepper

Remove the bones from the chops and roll each into a noisette. Tie firmly with string, or pass a short bamboo or metal skewer through each to hold it in shape. Rub with the garlic and onion, and set aside.

Heat the cooking oil in the wok and sauté the onion, ginger and garlic. Add the curry powder and sauté briefly. Add the tomato and coconut milk, bring to a boil and simmer for about 10 minutes. Then add the desiccated coconut and the seasonings and simmer for 5 to 6 minutes more. Pour into a bowl and set aside.

Rinse out the wok and dry thoroughly. Add about 1½ inches of oil to the wok and heat to moderate. Fry the noisettes in two or three batches until cooked through and golden brown (about 5 minutes), turning once. Remove and drain.

Pour off the oil. Return the noisettes to the wok and pour on the sauce. Heat gently for about 5 minutes, then serve.

Remove bones from chops and roll up

Rub the noisettes with garlic and onion

Add tomato and coconut milk

Lamb Cutlets with Mustard and Artichoke Sauce

Flatten the cutlets with a rolling pin

Add half the artichokes to sauce in a blender or food processor

Fry the cutlets in the butter and oil

SERVES 6

12 lamb cutlets★
½ cup seasoned
   flour
1 large egg, beaten
3 tablespoons milk
1 cup dry bread
   crumbs
3 tablespoons butter
3 tablespoons cooking oil

Sauce
2 tablespoons butter
1 medium onion,
   finely chopped
3 tablespoons flour
1 tablespoon Dijon
   mustard
¾ cup water
½ cup dry white wine
1 can artichoke hearts,
   drained
¾ cup heavy cream
2 teaspoons parsley,
   chopped
Salt and pepper

Pound the meaty part of each cutlet with the end of a rolling pin or a meat mallet to flatten and tenderize. Coat the cutlets lightly with the flour seasoned with salt and pepper. Beat the egg and milk together. Dip the cutlets into this mixture, then coat with the bread crumbs. Chill for about 45 minutes to set the crumbs.

To make the sauce, melt the butter in the wok and add the onion. Cook over low heat until the onion is transparent. Then sprinkle on the flour and cook briefly. Add the mustard and stir well, then add the water and wine and bring to a brisk boil. Whisk to remove any lumps, reduce heat and simmer for 1 to 2 minutes. Pour into a blender or food processor, add half the artichokes, and work to a smooth purée. Return the purée to the wok. Heat through, add the cream and parsley, and season to taste. Pour into a sauceboat and keep warm.

Rinse the wok and add the butter and oil. Heat until the butter foams, then add half the cutlets and fry for about 3 minutes on each side, until golden brown. Lift out with a slotted spoon and arrange on a warmed serving plate. Keep warm while the remaining cutlets are cooked. Drain the wok. Thinly slice the remaining artichoke hearts. Heat a little extra butter in the wok over low heat and lightly cook the artichoke hearts just until they are warmed through. Arrange over the cutlets and pour on a small amount of the sauce. Serve the remaining sauce separately.

★ *The cutlet bones should be decorated with a paper frill or covered with aluminum foil before serving.*

Pork Chops in Fruit Sauce

SERVES 6

6 pork chops
Salt and black pepper
1 egg white, lightly beaten
1 cup dry bread crumbs
½ cup butter

Fruit Sauce
1 (16-ounce) can black cherries with juice
2 cloves
½ teaspoon ground cinnamon
Grated rind of ¼ lemon
3½ tablespoons Madeira or Port

Season the chops with salt and pepper. Brush with the egg white and coat with the crumbs, shaking off excess. Chill for 1 hour to set the crumbs.

Melt the butter in the wok. Fry the chops, two or three at a time, until cooked through and golden brown (about 7 minutes). Lift out and keep warm while the remaining chops are cooked.

Blend half the fruit with the juice to a smooth purée, then heat in a small saucepan with the spices, lemon rind and wine. Simmer for 2 to 3 minutes.

When all the chops are cooked, return them all to the wok, pour on the sauce and remaining fruit and simmer gently for 4 to 5 minutes before serving. Alternatively, the sauce may be served separately.

Brush chops with egg white and coat with crumbs

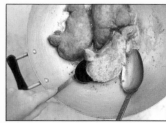

Fry 2-3 chops at a time until golden

Pour cherry sauce over chops in wok

Wiener Schnitzel

SERVES 6

This dish may be served in the traditional manner, by arranging overlapping steaks on a serving plate and garnishing them with lemon wedges, onion rings and drained capers. Alternatively, it may be served with Lemon and Mustard Hollandaise and slices of fresh avocado.

6 veal scallops
Freshly ground black pepper
2 tablespoons lemon juice
½ cup seasoned flour
2 large eggs, beaten
1¾ cups dry bread crumbs
5 tablespoons butter
5 tablespoons olive or cooking oil

Lemon and Mustard Hollandaise
3 egg yolks
Salt and pepper
1½ tablespoons lemon juice
1¾ tablespoons Dijon mustard
½ cup butter

Pound the scallops out very thinly, using a meat mallet or rolling pin and taking care not to break through at any point. Grind a little black pepper over one side of each scallop and sprinkle on the lemon juice. Leave for about 15 minutes.

Coat the scallops lightly with the seasoned flour, shaking off the excess. Dip into the beaten eggs, then coat with the crumbs. Arrange side by side on a tray and chill for 1 hour to set the crumbs.

Heat the butter with the olive or cooking oil in the wok. Fry the schnitzels three at a time, for about 3 minutes on each side. Drain thoroughly and keep warm while the remaining steaks are cooked.

To make the Lemon and Mustard Hollandaise, beat the egg yolks lightly with a dash of salt and pepper. Add the lemon juice and the Dijon mustard, and mix well. Place the bowl on a rack in the wok, and pour almost-boiling water into the wok.

Cut the butter into small cubes and slowly beat into the sauce, beating between each addition. When all the butter has been added, continue to beat gently until the sauce is thick and creamy. Do not allow the water to boil, or the sauce will curdle. Serve at once.

Note: Ask your butcher to thinly pound the veal scallops for you, if you prefer.

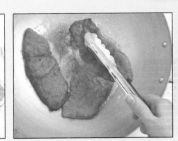

Season veal with pepper

Take care with coating when removing schnitzels

Gradually beat butter into sauce

Fritto Misto Milanese

SERVES 4

Many are familiar with the seafood version of Fritto Misto containing slivers of breaded fish, rings of calamari, scallops and shrimp, but this version from Milan is equally appetizing, with its combination of tender chicken breasts, brains and sweetbreads complemented by vegetables and soft Mozzarella cheese.

½ pound lamb's brains
½ pound sweetbreads
Salt
Juice of 1 lemon
½ pound chicken breasts
1 medium zucchini
¼ pound fresh mushrooms
3 ounces Mozzarella cheese
½ cup seasoned flour
2 eggs, beaten

1 cup dry bread crumbs
½ cup butter
2 to 3 tablespoons olive oil
1 tablespoon parsley, chopped

Soak the brains and sweetbreads separately in cold water for 1 hour. Drain, and pick off any membranes and specks of blood. Place in separate saucepans of cold water and add a dash of salt and lemon juice. Bring slowly to a boil and simmer for 15 to 18 minutes; then remove from the heat and leave to cool in the water. Remove and drain well.

Remove skin and any fragments of bone from the chicken and cut the meat into eight strips. Cut the brains and sweetbreads into eight pieces each. Wash, dry and slice the zucchini. Peel the mushrooms and trim the stems. Cut the cheese into four slices.

Prepare the seasoned flour (by adding salt and pepper). Coat the vegetables and meat with the flour; dip into the beaten egg; then coat with the crumbs. Arrange on a tray and chill for 1 hour.

Heat the butter and the olive oil in the wok to moderate. Fry the breaded meats and vegetables in small batches until tender. Remove with a slotted spoon, drain well on paper towels and arrange in groups on a well-heated serving plate. Keep warm until all ingredients have been cooked.

Drain the wok and wipe out any crumbs that have flaked off. Return the fat to the wok and reheat. Add the remaining lemon juice, heat until very foamy, then pour over the dish and garnish with the parsley. Serve at once.

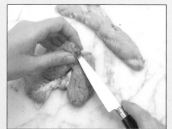
Remove membranes from sweetbreads and brains

Cut the cooled sweetbreads and brains into pieces

Coat vegetables and meat with flour

Chicken Akbar

SERVES 4

4 sheets Phyllo pastry
½ pound boneless chicken breasts
2 spring onions, chopped
1 small clove garlic, crushed
1 tablespoon pine nuts
1 tablespoon slivered almonds
2 tablespoons raisins
½ cup butter
1 teaspoon mild curry powder
1 tablespoon flour
3½ tablespoons chicken stock
3½ tablespoons heavy cream
Salt and black pepper

Cover the pastry with a paper towel until needed. Finely shred the chicken and mix with the onions and garlic.

Sauté the nuts and raisins with the chicken in one-third of the butter until the chicken is lightly browned. Sprinkle on the curry powder and cook briefly, then add the flour and cook for about 1 minute. Add the chicken stock and bring almost to a boil, stirring. Add the cream and seasoning, and simmer gently for about 2 minutes, until the sauce is thick. Remove from the heat and leave to cool slightly.

Fold each sheet of pastry in half to give rectangular shapes about 8 × 7 inches. Brush with the remaining butter, melted. Place one-quarter of the filling on each piece of pastry, fold in the sides and then fold the pastry over the filling to completely enclose it. Press the edges to seal.

Heat about ⅓ inch of mixed butter and oil in the wok and gently fry the pastries, two at a time, until golden. Drain and arrange on a serving plate. Serve hot.

Fold pastry in half and brush with butter

Place filling on pastry, fold in sides

Fold pastry over to enclose filling; press edges

Chicken Maryland

SERVES 4–6

While this name now seems to be applied to chicken in many forms—breaded and deep-fried, roasted or even battered and shallow-fried—the traditional recipe for Chicken Maryland states that it should be coated generously with well-seasoned flour, fried in bacon fat and served with accompanying fried bananas, grilled bacon and corn fritters. A tasty cream sauce made with the pan drippings is served with it.

2½ pounds chicken
1 cup flour
1 teaspoon salt
½ teaspoon black pepper
½ teaspoon oregano
½ teaspoon powdered
   sage
½ cup bacon fat or lard

Sauce
2 tablespoons flour
1 cup milk
3 tablespoons heavy
   cream
1 egg yolk, beaten
Salt and black pepper

Accompaniments
1 to 2 slices fatty
   bacon per serving
Sweet Corn Fritters
   (see page 61)
2 to 3 ripe but firm banana

Cut chicken into serving portions

Shallow-fry chicken pieces, several at a time, in wok until evenly browned

Cut the chicken into serving portions, trimming away and discarding the backbone. Mix the flour, salt, pepper and herbs together. Dip the chicken into the milk to be used for the sauce, then coat thickly with the seasoned flour.

Melt the fat or lard in the wok and, when moderately hot, fry the chicken, several pieces at a time, until well and evenly browned on the surface. Put in all the chicken, cover the wok and continue to cook gently for about 18 minutes, turning from time to time. Drain off the fat and remove the chicken.

Wipe out the wok to remove any flecks of burnt flour, then return about 2 tablespoons of the fat to the wok, to make the sauce. Add the flour, cook until lightly browned, then add the milk and stir on moderate heat until thickened. Remove from the heat. Beat the cream and egg yolk together and stir into the sauce. Add salt and pepper to taste, then return to low heat, stir until the sauce thickens, and keep it warm.

While the chicken is being cooked, grill the bacon separately until crisp. Corn fritters can be made in advance and reheated in the oven. Slice the peeled bananas, coat with the remaining seasoned flour and fry in the remainder of the cooking fat until crisp on the surface and soft inside. Surround the chicken with its accompaniments and serve hot with the sauce drizzled over.

Sweet and Sour Chicken Drumsticks

SERVES 3–6

6 chicken drumsticks
2 teaspoons light soy sauce
2 teaspoons dry sherry
1 teaspoon sugar
½ medium onion, thinly sliced
½ stick celery, thinly sliced diagonally
1 small carrot, thinly sliced
½ red pepper
1 (8-ounce) can sliced bamboo shoots, drained
3 slices fresh gingerroot, shredded
1 cup cornstarch
Cooking oil

Sauce
3½ tablespoons chicken stock
3½ tablespoons white vinegar
¼ cup sugar
½ teaspoon salt
1 teaspoon chili sauce or ground black pepper
2 to 3 drops red food coloring
1 tablespoon cornstarch

Prick the drumsticks all over and place in a dish. Add the soy sauce, sherry and sugar and rub thoroughly over the drumsticks. Leave for 20 minutes.

Prepare the vegetables. Cut the pepper into small squares, discarding the seed pod, stem and inner ribs. Mix the sauce ingredients together in a bowl and set aside.

Heat about 2 inches of cooking oil in the wok to moderately hot. Drain the drumsticks and coat thickly with the cornstarch, shaking off the excess. Fry until golden brown and cooked through (about 5 minutes), turning occasionally using tongs to prevent breaking the coating. Remove and drain on paper towels.

Pour off the oil, rinse out the wok and return about 2 tablespoons of the oil. Stir-fry the vegetables together for about 2½ minutes, then pour in the sauce and bring to a boil. Simmer, stirring, for 2 to 3 minutes. Return the drumsticks, and heat through. Serve at once.

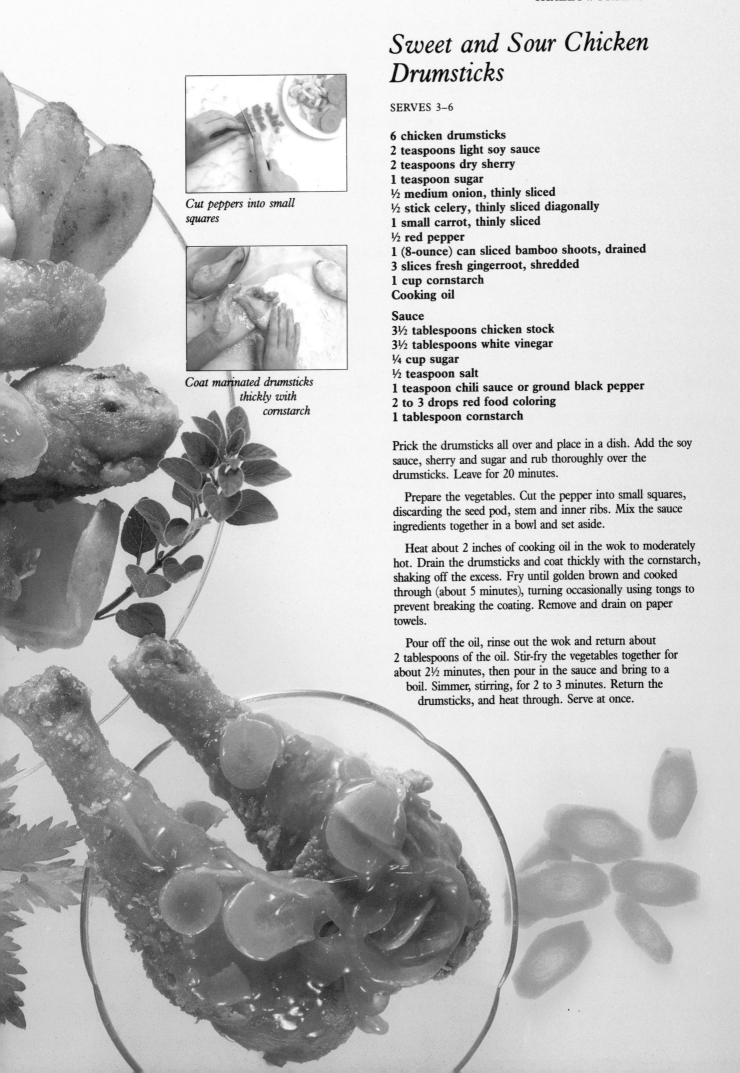

Cut peppers into small squares

Coat marinated drumsticks thickly with cornstarch

Thai-style Fish with Ginger Sauce

SERVES 6

This sauce is also suitable for serving with other seafoods or with plain fried chicken.

6 white fish fillets
¾ cup seasoned flour

Ginger Sauce
¼ pound ginger preserved in heavy syrup
1 tablespoon cornstarch
1 cup water
¼ cup sugar
3½ tablespoons white vinegar
1 tablespoon light soy sauce
Pinch of salt
2 to 3 spring onions, finely chopped

Dry the fish with paper towels and coat lightly with the seasoned flour. Set aside.

Finely chop the ginger. Place it in a wok or saucepan. Blend the cornstarch with a little of the water and add to wok with the remaining sauce ingredients; bring to a boil, stirring. Simmer for about 3 minutes, then set aside.

Wipe out the wok, if used, and add about 1½ inches of cooking oil. Fry the fish two pieces at a time, for about 3 minutes on each side, until cooked through. Lift out and drain. Cook the remaining fish. Arrange on a serving plate and pour on half the sauce. Serve the remaining sauce separately. Garnish with chili if liked.

Remove skin from fish fillets and coat with flour

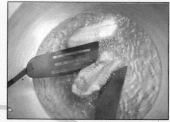

Fry the floured fish 2 pieces at a time

Pan-fried Fish with Green Mayonnaise

Sprinkle lemon juice over fish and coat with flour

Combine green mayonnaise ingredients

SERVES 4

8 small fillets of fish
⅓ cup flour
½ teaspoon salt
¼ teaspoon white pepper
1 tablespoon lemon juice
3 tablespoons butter
1 tablespoon cooking oil
1 lemon, thinly sliced
3 to 4 tablespoons parsley, chopped

Green Mayonnaise
2 hard-boiled eggs
1 cup mayonnaise
1 teaspoon Dijon or other French mustard
1 tablespoon raw spinach, finely chopped
1 tablespoon parsley, finely chopped
1 tablespoon drained capers, finely chopped

Dry the fish on paper towels. Mix the flour, salt and pepper together on a piece of paper. Sprinkle the lemon juice over the fish on both sides, then dip into the seasoned flour to coat evenly. Shake off the excess.

Heat the butter and cooking oil in the wok and fry two pieces of fish for about 2 minutes on each side, then for 1 more minute on the first side; remove and keep warm. Add additional butter and oil to the pan and fry the remaining fish.

Arrange the fish on a serving plate. Dip the sliced lemon into the chopped parsley and arrange over the fish. Pour on any butter that remains in the pan and serve at once.

To make the Green Mayonnaise, peel and finely chop the eggs or push through a wire sieve. Mix with the remaining sauce ingredients. If preferred, the sauce may be gently warmed before use. Leftover mayonnaise can be stored in an airtight jar in the refrigerator for up to a week and can be served with fish and shellfish.

Shrimp Stuffed with Crab

SERVES 4

1¼ pounds shrimp cutlets,*
2 teaspoons butter
1 tablespoon celery, finely chopped
1 tablespoon mushrooms, finely chopped
1 teaspoon fresh chili, finely chopped
1 tablespoon flour
3½ tablespoons milk
1½ teaspoons lemon juice
⅓ teaspoon salt
1 (6½-ounce) can crab meat, drained
2 cups fresh (soft) white bread crumbs
2 egg whites or 2 whole eggs

Heat the butter in the wok and sauté the celery, mushroom and chili briefly, then sprinkle in the flour and cook for about 30 seconds. Add the milk and bring to a boil; stir until the mixture is thick. Remove from the heat and add the lemon juice and salt. Stir in the crab meat and 1 tablespoon of the crumbs, and mix thoroughly to smooth any lumps. Cool. Stuff each of the shrimp cutlets with a spoonful of the filling, reforming them to their original shape. Chill for 1 hour.

Beat the egg whites or eggs in a dish. Spread the remaining crumbs on a piece of paper.

Heat about 1 inch of clean oil in the wok. Dip the shrimp in the beaten egg and coat evenly with the crumbs. Shallow-fry the shrimp, about four at a time, until golden brown and cooked through (about 3 minutes), turning once. Drain on paper towels and keep warm while the remainder are cooked. Serve hot.

*Peeled raw shrimp with the tail shell left on, deveined and butterflied (slit open down the center of the back and pressed open)

Stuff each shrimp with crab mixture

Dip shrimp in beaten egg whites and coat with crumbs

Honey Nut Pastries

Plakoundes

MAKES 18

6 sheets Phyllo pastry
⅓ cup butter
¼ cup sugar
5 tablespoons water
2 teaspoons honey
1½ teaspoons lemon juice
1 small strip lemon rind
Clarified butter for frying

Filling
½ cup almonds, coarsely ground
1 egg yolk
2 tablespoons sugar
¾ teaspoon ground cinnamon
¼ teaspoon grated nutmeg

Thaw the pastry, if frozen, and keep wrapped in a paper towel until needed. Melt the butter and set aside.

Boil the sugar, water, honey and lemon juice together for 2 minutes. Add the lemon rind and continue to boil until syrupy (5 to 6 more minutes), then set aside to cool.

Mix the filling ingredients together. Cut the pastry sheets lengthwise into three even-sized strips. Brush lightly with the melted butter and fold each in half to give pieces about 8 × 4 inches. Brush one side with more butter and place a spoonful of the filling toward one end. Fold the two sides in about ¾ inch and fold the bottom over the filling. Then roll up tightly, brushing a little more butter on the end flap before pressing into place.

When all the pastries are rolled, heat about 1 inch of clarified butter in the wok over moderate heat. Fry the pastries, about six at a time, until golden. Place in the pan with the end flaps downward at first to prevent them unrolling during cooking. Turn carefully using two large spoons.

When they're golden on both sides, drain well on paper towels and arrange on a plate. Pour on the syrup and leave to cool before serving.

Cut pastry into strips; keep remainder covered

Fill pastries and roll up tightly

Strawberry Cream Puffs

MAKES 36

¼ cup butter
1¼ cups milk
Rind of 1 lemon, grated
2 teaspoons sugar
¼ teaspoon salt
¾ cup flour
4 large eggs
1 cup whipped
   cream
1 pint fresh strawberries
Confectioners' sugar

Place the butter in a saucepan and melt gently without allowing it to bubble. Add the milk and the grated lemon rind, and bring to a boil; simmer for 3 minutes. Add the sugar and salt and then quickly work in the flour, stirring with a wooden spoon; cook, stirring constantly, over moderate heat for about 5 minutes. Remove from the heat and beat in the eggs one at a time. Make sure each egg is fully incorporated into the mixture before you add the next one. The dough should be smooth and shiny.

Heat about 2 inches clean cooking oil in the wok to moderate. Drop in teaspoonfuls of the mixture and fry for 4 to 6 minutes until golden and puffed, turning several times during cooking. The oil must not be allowed to overheat or the pastries will cook on the outside while the inside will remain sticky and undercooked. Drain the cooked cream puffs and allow to cool.

When cool, slit on one side with a sharp knife. Fill each with whipped cream and add half a strawberry to each, allowing the point of the berry to protrude from the slit. Dust lightly with confectioners' sugar and serve.

Beat eggs, one at a time into cooked dough

Drop teaspoonfuls of mixture into hot oil

Pineapple Fritters

SERVES 6

1 medium-sized fresh pineapple
½ cup flour
2 tablespoons almonds, chopped
½ cup water
Pinch of salt
1 tablespoon sugar
1 teaspoon baking powder
2 egg whites
Confectioners' sugar

Peel the pineapple and cut into six thick slices. Place on a double thickness of paper towels, and cover with more towels. Leave to absorb as much of the juice as possible.

Sift the flour into a mixing bowl and add the almonds, water, salt, sugar and baking powder. Beat until smooth.

Heat about 1½ inches clarified butter or clean cooking oil in the wok to moderately hot. Beat the egg whites to soft peaks, then fold them into the batter. Dip the pineapple into the batter and place in the oil. Fry two or three pieces at a time until golden brown. Lift out and drain well on paper towels. Keep cooked fritters warm in a low oven with the door ajar.

Sprinkle with confectioners' sugar and serve hot with vanilla ice cream or whipped cream.

Thick slices of apple, cored but unpeeled, can be used instead of the pineapple. Or try ripe but firm bananas, halved lengthwise.

Peel pineapple and cut into thick slices

Press slices with paper towel to absorb juice

Poaching

Poaching is a simple, effective cooking technique, which is largely overlooked in the home kitchen. It is the gentle cooking of foods in a liquid that remains at a temperature just below the boil. This is described as "gently boiling" or "barely simmering." The objective is to cook gently and slowly so that the food retains its natural composition and shape, becomes well flavored with the liquid in which it is being cooked, and retains all of its own natural moisture.

Poaching is used particularly for foods of a delicate texture, such as fish and other seafood, poultry, the soft offal (brains and sweetbreads), firm fresh fruits and certain vegetables.

The stock used for poaching varies according to the dish and the seasonings added. It may be a classic *court bouillon* using diced vegetables, herbs and seasonings in a stock of dry white wine and water; a simple chicken or veal stock; a flavored wine; or simply water enhanced with spices, citrus juices, sugar and liqueurs. The well-flavored poaching liquid is often served with the dish as a sauce or a soup. It may be reused in certain cases for preparing another similar dish.

The large capacity of the wok, with its sloped sides, makes it an excellent poaching pan for foods as small as a pair of quails or a peach, or as large as a whole fish or joint of meat.

Although it differs in shape from the traditional elongated oval-shaped fish poacher, the wok serves this purpose well. Fish poachers are fitted with an internal basket, which can be removed from the pan and which prevents the tender fish breaking up after it is cooked. In the wok, the fish can rest on a perforated metal or wire mesh rack, which will hold it above the center bottom of the wok to prevent the possibility of spot-burning. It can be slipped out of the wok with fish intact after cooking. Chickens, ducks and small birds such as quails can also be poached on a rack or in a frying basket to make it easier to remove the tender cooked dish from the wok.

Generally, the poaching liquid will be prepared in advance and simmered for some time to extract the full flavor from its ingredients. It is then strained into the wok and heated before the food is added.

When meats are being poached to render them tender, as in the case of brains or sweetbreads or salt pork, they will be placed in the wok and covered with cold water, brought to poaching temperature and then left to cook gently until ready. This liquid is not retained for use as a soup or sauce.

Firm fresh fruit such as peaches, pears and plums can be transformed into exotic desserts by simply poaching in flavored liquid, usually a combination of wine and sugar. The cooking liquid will thicken and caramelize during the cooking and is served with the fruit. If necessary, a thin sauce may be thickened slightly by the addition of a mixture of cornstarch and cold water.

Dried fruits may be poached as well, either in water with sugar added to sweeten, or in sweetened wine or liqueurs. A handful of dried prunes, apricots and figs poached with water and a can of cherries (Hot Fruit Compote) makes a quick

Thai Shrimp in Chili and Lime Soup

Tom Yam Kung

SERVES 6

This is most impressive cooked at the table in a Chinese steamboat or a fondue pot.

1½ pounds uncooked shrimp, in the shell
6½ cups fish stock
1 lime, quartered
4 lime leaves
2 stalks lemon grass, sliced in halves
2 cloves garlic, sliced
2 fresh red chilies, sliced
1 tablespoon fish sauce (*nam pla*)*
1 teaspoon chili sauce (optional)
Salt and black pepper
4 to 6 spring onions, finely chopped
Additional lime juice

Wash the shrimp in cold water. Do not remove the shells. If desired, slit down the center of the backs to remove the dark vein.

Bring the fish stock to a gentle boil. Add the lime, lime leaves, lemon grass (white root end only), garlic and chilies, and simmer for 10 to 12 minutes. Add the fish sauce, chili sauce, salt and pepper to taste, and simmer for 10 to 12 more minutes.

The shrimp should be added about 7 minutes before serving time and gently poached in the piquant stock. Add the onions, and extra lime juice to taste just before serving.

*A product from Thailand or Vietnam. If unobtainable use light soy sauce.

Add lime, leaves, chili and lemon grass to stock

Add shrimp to the well-flavored stock

Mussels in Wine

Moules Marinière

SERVES 6

Mussel enthusiasts shun the use of a spoon and use instead one of the mussel shells to scoop up the delicious wine and cream-based soup in which these mussels are cooked and served. A bib is recommended.

3½ pounds fresh mussels
2 spring onions, chopped
½ stick celery, chopped
1 tablespoon parsley, chopped
2 cups dry white wine
1 cup water
1 bouquet garni (bunch of fresh herbs)
¼ teaspoon freshly ground black pepper
Pinch of salt
3 tablespoons heavy cream
2 teaspoons butter
2 teaspoons flour

Thoroughly wash the mussels, scrubbing the shells with a hard brush to remove any barnacles. Pull away the beards. Rinse in clean cold water.

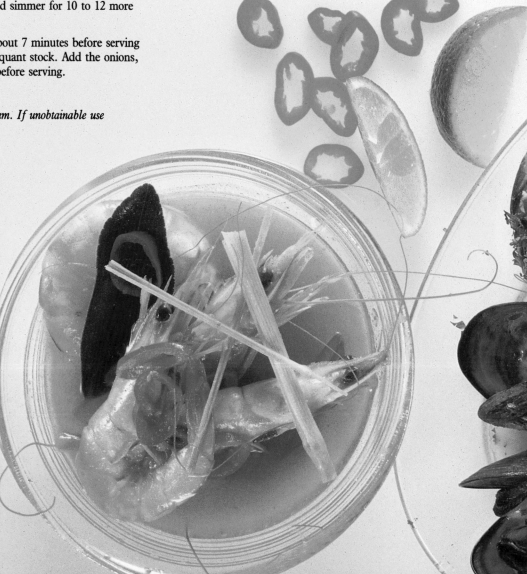

Place the onions and celery in the wok with half the parsley, and the wine, water, herbs, pepper and salt. Bring to a boil and boil briskly for 2 to 3 minutes.

Add the mussels, cover and cook for about 8 minutes until the mussels open. Shake the pan from time to time. Discard any mussels that do not open. Remove the mussels to a deep serving dish using a slotted spoon.

Return the liquid to the boil and discard the herbs. Mix the cream with the butter and flour, working to a smooth thin paste; pour into the wok and whisk until well blended. Add the remaining parsley and check for salt. Pour over the mussels and serve at once.

Duck Poached with Lemons and Limes

SERVES 6–8 AS AN APPETIZER

This may also be served to 4 to 6 people as a main course with other Chinese dishes.

3 pounds duck
1 lemon
1 lime
1 large spring onion, trimmed
3 thin slices fresh gingerroot
1½ teaspoons salt

Cut the duck into serving pieces and place in the wok. Quarter the lemon and lime without peeling, and arrange around the duck. Add the whole onion and the ginger slices, the salt and water to cover. Cover the wok and bring the water just to a boil, then reduce heat and simmer with the water just barely boiling for about 1¾ hours until the duck is very tender.

Skim the fat from the surface and serve the duck in its soup, or serve meat and soup separately if preferred.

Scrub mussels and pull away the beards

Mussels open when cooked

Using poultry shears, cut duck into serving pieces.

Place duck in wok and simmer with fruit

Veal with Tunafish Sauce

Vitello Tonnato

SERVES 6–8

2 pounds veal roast (loin
   or shoulder)
2 fillets of anchovy
1½ teaspoons salt
Freshly ground black
   pepper
1 medium onion
2 cloves
1 bay leaf
1 stick celery
1 medium carrot
2 to 3 sprigs parsley

Sauce
1 (6½-ounce) can tuna,
   drained
2 fillets of anchovy
½ cup olive oil
1 to 2 lemons
1 tablespoon capers,
   drained

*Pierce veal and insert pieces
of anchovy*

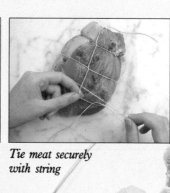

*Tie meat securely
with string*

*Very slowly add oil to the
tuna mixture until sauce is
smooth and thick*

Pierce the veal with the point of a knife at intervals and
insert small pieces of anchovy. Season the meat with salt and
pepper. Roll it up, tie securely with string, and place in the
wok. Peel the onion and stud it with the cloves.
Add it and the remaining ingredients to the wok. Add warm
water to cover the meat; cover the wok and bring to a
boil, then reduce the heat and leave to simmer gently for
about 1½ hours.

Remove the meat from the wok and leave to cool,
covered with a clean cloth.

Place the tuna in a food processor or blender with the
anchovy and then gradually add the olive oil, blending at
moderate speed until the oil has all been incorporated
and the sauce is smooth and thick. Squeeze the juice
from the lemons and add to the sauce to taste. Add the
capers, whole or finely chopped.

Untie the veal and slice thinly. Arrange overlapped
on a serving plate. Pour on the sauce and garnish with
twists of lemon.

This dish is even more delicious if it is prepared about 6
hours in advance to allow time for the
flavors of the sauce to penetrate the meat.

Chicken in Soy Sauce

SERVES 4–6

1 (2½-pound) roasting chicken
5 spring onions, trimmed
5 thick slices fresh gingerroot
1 teaspoon sesame oil (optional)
2 Chinese star anise

Sauce
2 cups chicken stock or water
1 cup light soy sauce
½ cup dark soy sauce
½ cup sugar

Clean the chicken and wipe with paper towels. Into the cavity, put 2 onions and 2 slices of ginger. Rub the skin with the sesame oil, if used. Place the chicken in the wok on a small oiled rack to hold it just above the bottom of the wok. Place the star anise and remaining onions and ginger in the wok on either side of the chicken.

Add the sauce ingredients and bring to a gentle boil. Cover the wok, reduce the heat and simmer slowly with the bubbles just occasionally breaking the surface, until the chicken is completely tender (about 50 minutes). Turn once to ensure even cooking.

Lift the chicken out of the stock with two slotted spoons and drain thoroughly. Cut into serving pieces and serve hot with a little of the poaching liquid as a sauce.

The remaining liquid can be reused for another chicken. A sliced fresh red chili and a piece of orange or tangerine peel can be added to the poaching liquid for added flavor.

Place chicken on rack or chopsticks in wok

Add star anise, onion and ginger

Add sauce, cover and simmer

Poached Whole Fish

Add fish to court bouillon in wok

Sauté mushrooms until softened

Scrape skin away from cooked fish

SERVES 4

2 pounds fresh fish (sea trout or sea bass)

Court Bouillon
4 cups water
1½ cups dry white wine
1½ teaspoons salt
1 medium onion, sliced
⅓ stalk celery, sliced
1 medium carrot, sliced
1 clove garlic, lightly crushed
5 black peppercorns
1 clove
1 bay leaf
Rind of ½ lemon
1 sprig each fresh fennel, thyme and parsley

Tomato and Mushroom Sauce
1 cup fresh button mushrooms, sliced
¼ cup butter
1 tablespoon flour
2 egg yolks
3 tablespoons heavy cream
1 teaspoon tomato paste or purée

Clean and scale the fish and wash in cold water. Set aside.

Place the ingredients for the court bouillon in the wok and bring to a boil. Cover and simmer for 25 minutes.

Add the fish, reduce the heat, and allow the fish to simmer very gently with the liquid just barely boiling, for about 20 minutes.

Lift out the fish using two spatulas, transfer it to a warmed serving dish, cover and keep warm. Reserve and strain the court bouillon.

Sauté the mushrooms in half the butter until softened. Remove from the wok. Add the remaining butter and the flour, and cook, stirring, over moderate heat until it is lightly browned. Add about 1½ cups of the reserved stock and bring to a boil; stir over moderate heat until thickened. Remove from the heat and stir in the egg yolks and the cream and tomato paste. Beat for 1 minute, then add the mushrooms and heat through.

Carefully scrape the skin from the fish and cover the fish with the sauce. Serve at once.

Poached fish is also delicious served cold and is an ideal dish for a light lunch or on a cold buffet table. After scraping away the skin, cover the fish with a thin coating of mayonnaise and decorate it with narrow strips of red and green pepper and rolled anchovies or strips of black olive.

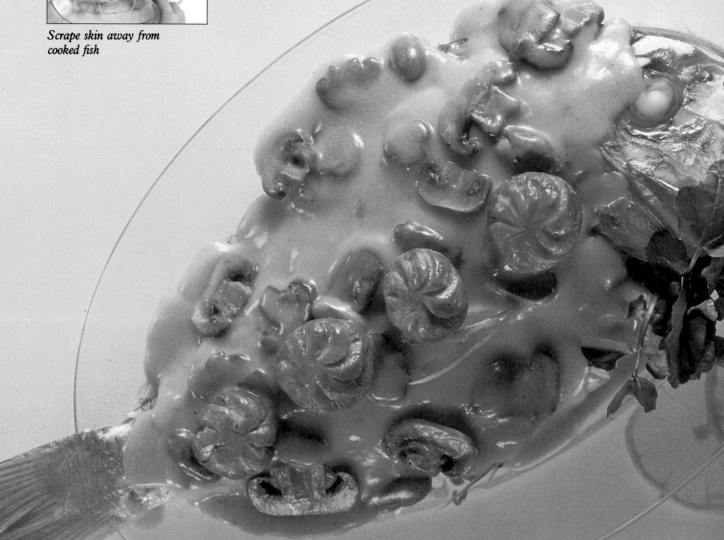

Sole Véronique

SERVES 6

This light and creamy fish dish can also be served as an appetizer or second (fish) course. Presented on a bed of white or saffron rice, it should serve 8 to 10.

1½ pounds fillets of sole or other small fish fillets
1 cup water
¾ cup dry white wine
6 black peppercorns
1 large spring onion, trimmed
¼ pound seedless green grapes
Lemon juice

Sauce
1 tablespoon butter
3 tablespoons flour
¼ cup milk
3 to 4 tablespoons heavy cream
2 egg yolks, beaten

Wash the fillets and dry on paper towels. Fold each piece in half and arrange in a well-buttered dish that will fit inside the wok. Add the water, wine, peppercorns and spring onion, and cover the dish with a piece of buttered parchment. Set on a rack in the wok, add water to the level of the rack and cover. Bring the water to a boil and steam the fish over moderately high heat for about 12 minutes.

When done, transfer the fish to a warmed serving plate. Cover with foil and keep it warm in a low oven with the door ajar while you make the sauce. Reserve and strain 1¼ cups of the poaching liquid.

Peel the grapes and cut into halves. Sprinkle with a little lemon juice and set aside.

Melt the butter in a clean wok and add the flour. Cook briefly, then pour in the milk and the reserved stock. Stir until the sauce boils and thickens slightly (about 2 minutes), then remove from the heat. Mix the cream and egg yolks together and add to the sauce. Beat until smooth, then return to low heat to cook until the sauce is thick and creamy. Stir continually to prevent burning or curdling.

Add the grapes, then pour the sauce over the fish.

Cover fish with buttered paper

Peel and halve grapes, remove seeds

Pears in Red Wine

SERVES 6

6 ripe but firm pears
½ cup sugar
1½ cups red wine
1½ cups water
1 tablespoon vanilla sugar* or
**   1 teaspoon vanilla extract**
1 tablespoon cornstarch

Peel the pears and set aside. Mix the sugar, wine and water together in the wok and bring to a boil, stirring until the sugar is dissolved.

Add the pears and vanilla and reduce the heat. Partially cover the wok and gently poach the pears for about 1¼ hours, until they are very tender but still holding their shape. The syrup should be reduced to 1¼ cups.

Use a slotted spoon to lift the pears from the wok and transfer to glass dessert dishes.

Mix the cornstarch with an equal amount of cold water and slowly stir into the syrup. Stir on moderate heat until the sauce is thick and transparent. Spoon over the pears. Serve hot with whipped cream.

* *Finely ground sugar with the flavor of vanilla*
—made by storing a vanilla pod in a jar of sugar.
If unobtainable, substitute 1 teaspoon of vanilla extract.

Add pears to wine syrup in wok

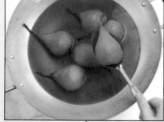
Lift cooked pears out of syrup with a slotted spoon

Vanilla pods give a superb flavor to sugar

Apricot Delight

Mishmisheya

SERVES 6

This smooth purée of dried apricots, highlighted by the crunchy texture of almonds and the hint of orange-flavored liqueur, is typical of the extravagant sweet dishes from the Middle East. Sour cream can be served as the accompaniment for those who prefer a less rich dessert.

1 box dried apricots
½ cup sugar
⅓ cup blanched almonds
1 cup heavy cream
3 tablespoons sugar
1 tablespoon Cointreau or Grand Marnier
2 tablespoons toasted almonds, chopped

Wash the apricots and place in the wok with water to cover. Bring almost to a boil and poach gently for 30 minutes.

Add the sugar and stir until dissolved, then remove from the heat and allow to cool slightly.

Transfer to a blender or food processor and work to a smooth purée. Stir in the blanched almonds, which have been cut into slivers, then chill thoroughly.

Whip the cream, adding the sugar and liqueur. Spoon the apricot purée into a glass serving dish and top with the whipped cream and the toasted almonds.

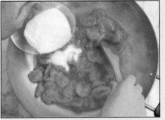

Add sugar to poached dried apricots in wok

Purée the poached dried apricots

Stir in the slivered almonds

Floating Islands in Blackberry Sauce

SERVES 4

1 (16-ounce) can blackberries
½ teaspoon salt
2 egg whites
1 tablespoon sugar

Pour the blackberries and their liquid into a blender and purée, then pass through a fine sieve to remove the seeds. Heat gently and set aside.

Bring about 6½ cups of water to a gentle boil in the wok and add the salt.

Beat the egg whites until stiff, add the sugar and continue to beat until it stands in firm peaks and is very shiny. Take tablespoons of the mixture and drop into the water. Poach, about six at a time, for 4 to 5 minutes on one side, then flip over and cook on the other side for the same time. Remove the meringues with a slotted spoon.

Reheat the berry purée gently, then pour into a wide shallow serving dish. Float the meringues on top. Serve as soon as the last batch are cooked.

Lightly sweetened cream can accompany this light and tangy dessert.

Sieve the puréed black-berries to remove seeds

Beat egg whites and sugar until they stand in peaks

Drop meringue into water and poach

Hot Fruit Compote

SERVES 6

1 (16-ounce) can stoned black cherries in syrup
¼ cup dried apricots
½ cup dessert prunes
¼ cup dried figs
2½ cups water

Place the fruit and liquid from the cherries in the wok and add the water. Cover and bring almost to a boil, then poach gently for about 1½ hours until the fruit is tender and the liquid well reduced. The cherry liquid should provide enough sugar to sweeten the dish.

Serve hot in small glass dishes with a generous topping of whipped cream.

Place fruit and cherry syrup in wok with water

Poach until fruit is tender

Prunes and Oranges in Port

SERVES 6-8

1 box dessert prunes
2 large sweet oranges
5 cloves
1 cinnamon stick
¾ cup port
2½ cups water
½ cup sugar

Wash the prunes and soak for 2 hours, then drain well.

Use a sharp knife to thickly peel the oranges, ensuring that all pith is removed. Separate each segment of orange, cutting away all membranes. Reserve a strip of the rind for use in the dish, and scrape away its pith.

Place the prunes, oranges and reserved orange rind in the wok with the remaining ingredients. Cover and poach gently until the prunes are tender. Serve hot or cold with fresh or whipped cream.

Peel all skin and pith from oranges

Separate oranges into segments

Add port to fruit, sugar and spices

Steaming

Steaming as a cooking method was discovered by the Chinese many centuries ago. Chefs, regarding the applying of fire directly to foods as a barbarian practice, sought various methods to introduce an intermediary between food and the cooking pot. Frying and sautéeing became popular, but it was the purity of steaming that had the most appeal.

Not that steaming remained the exclusive right of Chinese cooks. For centuries the British have relied on steaming for their delicious puddings, both sweet and savory. And as health-consciousness increasingly influences cooking styles around the world, cooks are turning to steaming as a simple and unrivaled way to prepare light, low-calorie and delicious meals.

Steam is no more than the result of the meeting of those two old antagonists, fire and water. But steam is hotter than water can ever be—once water has reached the boil at 212°F, it requires additional heat before it can vaporize into steam. The steam quickly permeates whatever is being cooked, keeping the moisture in. Therefore, steam cooks more thoroughly and rapidly than any other technique. It saves time, and time means money when gas, electricity or other valuable fuels are being used. The problems of burning and overcooking are virtually eliminated with steaming and, as a method of reheating food, steaming is invaluable.

The wok is an ideal steaming vessel. The various bamboo, metal or wire racks made to accompany the wok are designed to fit into its curved bottom allowing space below for the water. The food to be cooked is placed in a dish on this rack and the wok lid set in place above. This fits snugly inside the rim of the wok. Steaming baskets of various sizes are also used with the wok. Smaller ones stand on a rack inside the wok and are covered with the lid, while larger ones sit directly inside the rim of the wok and their own lids are used to cover. These are used particularly for the many snack-like dishes of which the Chinese are specialists, but they are now being put to good use in the cooking of a variety of dishes.

For successful steaming, ensure that the wok sits firmly over the heat source—in this instance gas or electricity is equally effective. Choose a rack that allows about 2 inches of space beneath and add water to the level of the rack. Place the food in a dish with sides high enough to contain the cooking liquids plus the quantity of extra liquid that will be added to the pan through the process of condensation during the cooking—the steam will condense on the inside of the lid and drop into the dish. The wok lid should fit snugly inside the rim of the wok. To prevent leakage, place a twisted dish towel around the edge of the lid, making sure that no parts come in contact with the heat source.

The water should be brought to a rapid boil, then the heat regulated in accordance with the needs of the particular dish, i.e. high, moderate, gentle, etc. as explained in each recipe. All that needs to be done through the cooking is to ensure that the water level does not drop much below the level of the rack.

A warning note: steam, as we've already mentioned, is very hot. Wear a pair of thick oven gloves or protect the hands with a cloth when removing a dish from a steamer. And always lift the back of the lid first to direct the cloud of released steam away from hands and face.

Scallop Mousseline in Saffron Sauce

SERVES 6

1 pound fresh scallops
2 teaspoons lemon juice
2 eggs
1 tablespoon flour
3 teaspoons cornstarch
3 tablespoons fish stock
Salt and pepper
1 spring onion, chopped

Saffron Sauce
½ cup milk
¼ teaspoon saffron powder
¼ teaspoon mustard powder
⅓ teaspoon salt
1 tablespoon butter
2½ teaspoons flour
½ cup light cream
2 egg yolks

Marinate the scallops in the lemon juice for 10 minutes. Transfer to a food processor or blender, and purée to a smooth paste. Add the remaining ingredients and purée again until smooth. Pour into six buttered, individual, heatproof dishes and cover each with a piece of buttered aluminum foil.

Set on a rack in the wok and add water to the level of the rack. Bring to a boil, then steam gently for about 25 minutes until set.

Turn out onto medium-sized plates and coat with the sauce. Garnish each plate with a cooked shrimp or poached scallop with the roe attached, and a sprig of coriander.

To make the Saffron Sauce, scald the milk in a small saucepan with the saffron, mustard and salt. Remove from the heat and set aside.

Melt the butter in another pan. Add the flour and cook, stirring, for 1 minute. Pour in the milk and bring to a boil, stirring; simmer for 2 minutes, then remove from the heat.

Beat the cream and egg yolks together and pour into the pan. Beat until the sauce is smooth, then return to low heat and cook gently until the sauce thickens (about 3 minutes), stirring constantly.

Pour the puréed scallop mixture into dishes

Cover dishes with foil and place on a rack in the wok

Carefully turn out the cooked mousseline

Steamed Stuffed Jumbo Shrimp

SERVES 6 AS AN APPETIZER, 4 AS A MAIN COURSE

12 raw large shrimp, in the shell

Seasoning
½ teaspoon salt
½ teaspoon sugar
¼ teaspoon white pepper
½ teaspoon sesame oil (optional)
2 teaspoons light soy sauce
1 tablespoon spring onions, finely chopped
2 teaspoons fresh gingerroot, grated

Wash the shrimp and use a sharp knife to cut through the shells along the backs; pick out the intestinal veins and rinse the shrimp in cold water. Mix the remaining ingredients together and insert a little into the cut section of each shrimp, pressing down well.

Place the shrimp on an oiled plate and set on a rack in the wok. Cover tightly and steam briskly for 8 minutes. Serve with steamed rice.

Cut shrimp along the back and remove the vein   *Insert seasonings into each cut section*

Egg Custard with Shrimp

SERVES 4

½ pound raw shrimp, peeled
½ teaspoon salt
1 tablespoon dry sherry or ginger wine
1 teaspoon ginger, finely chopped
6 large eggs
1 large spring onion, finely chopped
¾ teaspoon salt
Pinch of pepper

Wash the shrimp and drain well. Place in a dish and season with the ½ teaspoon of salt, sherry and ginger; leave for 10 minutes, then pour off excess liquid.

Lightly beat the eggs, adding the onion, salt and pepper. Divide the shrimp between four individual, heatproof, covered dishes and pour the egg mixture on top.

Set on a rack in the wok and steam over gently boiling water for 12 minutes, or until firm. Do not overcook.

Pour the egg mixture into heatproof bowls on top of the shrimp   *Cover with foil and steam in a basket or on a rack in the wok*

Stuffed Grape Leaves
Dolmades

MAKES 48

1 package of grape leaves in brine
¼ pound ground beef
1 medium onion, chopped
3 tablespoons olive oil
2 cloves garlic, chopped
3 large tomatoes
3 tablespoons parsley, chopped
3 tablespoons celery leaves, chopped
3 tablespoons almonds, chopped
1 cup raw long-grain rice
1 cup tomato juice

Drain the grape leaves, cover with boiling water and leave for 20 minutes. Drain and rinse in fresh boiling water and cover with cold water until needed.

Sauté the beef, onion and garlic lightly in a little of the olive oil. Finely chop 1 tomato and add to the pan along with the parsley, celery and almonds. Sauté briefly, mixing well.

Cover the rice with boiling water and leave to stand for 1 minute; then drain thoroughly and add to the meat mixture.

Drain the grape leaves and fill each with a teaspoon of the mixture, placing it on the ribbed side of the leaves.

Fold over the stem section first, then the two sides, and roll up toward the pointed end of the leaf. Arrange closely together, seams downward, in a lightly oiled dish. Pour on the tomato juice and the remaining olive oil. Slice the remaining tomatoes and place over the grape-leaf rolls. Top with any remaining grape leaves.

Set on a rack in the wok, add water to the level of the rack, cover the wok and steam for about 1¼ hours until the rice has expanded and become tender. Check the level of the water every 15 minutes and add more if needed. It may be necessary to add a little more tomato juice during cooking as it becomes absorbed.

Serve the Dolmades warm or cold, with a dressing of olive oil and plain yogurt or sour cream.

Drain grape leaves and cover with boiling water

Add soaked and drained rice to sautéed beef

Place the filling on ribbed side of leaves

Roll up and place on an oiled plate, then steam

Cabbage Rolls

MAKES 12

3 pounds cabbage
¾ pound coarsely
    ground pork
1 large onion, chopped
1 large tomato, chopped
3 tablespoons butter
1½ tablespoons flour
1½ teaspoons sweet
    paprika
Salt and black pepper
2 teaspoons parsley,
    chopped
¼ teaspoon dried oregano
1 egg, beaten

Tomato Sauce
1 medium onion, finely
    chopped
1 large tomato, chopped
1 clove garlic, crushed
1 tablespoon butter
½ teaspoon sugar
Salt and black pepper
½ cup heavy
    cream

Separate the cabbage leaves and select 12 large ones for the rolls. Trim away the central stems. Place the leaves and about ½ cup of the remaining cabbage in the wok. Cover with boiling water and simmer gently for about 5 minutes until the leaves have softened. Drain well.

Wipe out the wok, then fry the pork, onion and tomato in the butter for about 5 minutes, stirring frequently. Add the flour and paprika, salt and pepper to taste, and the herbs. Cover and simmer gently for 5 to 6 minutes. Remove from the heat and leave to cool for about 10 minutes.

Stir the egg into the pork mixture. Chop the blanched excess cabbage finely, squeeze to remove as much water as possible, and mix into the pork mixture.

Divide the filling between the 12 prepared leaves and roll up each to enclose the filling. Place in a dish, seams downward, and set on a rack in a clean wok. Add water to the level of the rack and steam, tightly covered, for about 45 minutes. Add more water as needed.

In a separate saucepan or wok, prepare the sauce by sautéeing the onion, tomato and garlic in the butter until soft. Add the sugar, salt and pepper to taste, and simmer gently until thick. Stir in the cream just before using.

To serve the cabbage rolls, drain and arrange on a plate. Pour on the sauce.

Cover cabbage with boiling water, then cook

Divide filling among leaves and roll up

Cover and steam in a dish on rack in wok

Cucumber with Pork Stuffing

SERVES 6

1 large cucumber
½ pound lean pork, finely minced
1 large spring onion, chopped
2 slices fresh gingerroot, chopped
2 teaspoons light soy sauce
¾ teaspoon dry sherry
¾ teaspoon sugar
1 teaspoon cornstarch

Sauce
2 teaspoons light soy sauce
2 teaspoons Chinese oyster sauce
1 teaspoon cornstarch

Wipe the cucumber and remove the ends, then cut into six thick slices. Use a small knife to remove the seed core, making each piece of cucumber into a ring.

Mix the pork with the remaining ingredients and use to fill the cucumber rings. Set on a lightly oiled plate. Place the plate on a rack in the wok and add water to just below the rack. Cover and steam gently for about 25 minutes.

Drain the liquid from the plate into a clean wok and add the other sauce ingredients. Bring to a boil and stir for about 1 minute, then pour over the cucumbers and serve.

Pork Dumplings

Siew Mai

MAKES 18

½ pound fatty pork
2 dried Chinese mushrooms, soaked
1 spring onion, chopped
½ teaspoon fresh gingerroot, grated
2 teaspoons parsley, chopped
½ egg white, beaten
¾ teaspoon salt
1 teaspoon sugar
1½ teaspoons light soy sauce
½ teaspoon dark soy sauce
1 tablespoon cornstarch
2 to 3 tablespoons green peas
1 small carrot
18 fresh or frozen wonton wrappers

Cut the pork into small pieces and place in a food processor or blender. Grind to a smooth paste, then transfer to a dish. Squeeze the water from the mushrooms, remove stems and chop the caps finely. Mix all the ingredients, except peas, carrot and wrappers, together with the pork, kneading until thoroughly mixed and a sticky paste. Cover with plastic wrap and chill for 1 hour.

Parboil the peas and the carrot, which has been cut into very small dice. Drain and set aside.

Cut cucumber into thick slices and remove seeds

Fill cucumber with meat mixture; set on plate

Thaw and separate the wrappers, trim off the four corners, then cover with a cloth until needed.

To form the dumplings, place 2 teaspoonfuls of the mixture in the center of each wrapper and fold the wrapper up and around the sides. Press it firmly onto the filling, leaving the top open. Place 2 peas and a cube of carrot on the top of each dumpling and press lightly into the filling.

Set the dumplings into a lightly greased steaming basket or on an oiled wire cake cooler, and set on a rack in the wok.

Add water to below the level of the rack to prevent the boiling water touching the dumplings. Cover, bring to a boil and steam for about 12 minutes until cooked through. Serve straight from the steamer with dips of hot mustard and soy sauce.

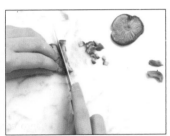

Remove stems from soaked and squeezed mushrooms and chop caps finely

Press wrapping firmly around filling to form a dumpling

Chinese Pork Buns
Cha Siew Pow

MAKES 12

Dough
2½ cups flour
1 tablespoon baking powder
⅓ cup sugar
1 tablespoon softened lard
½ cup lukewarm water

Filling
¼ pound Chinese roast pork
   or smoked ham
1 large spring onion, chopped
1 tablespoon vegetable oil
2 teaspoons light soy sauce
1 teaspoon dark soy sauce
1 teaspoon Chinese oyster sauce
1 tablespoon sugar
1 teaspoon dry sherry
¼ cup water
1 tablespoon cornstarch

Sift the flour and baking powder into a mixing bowl. Add the sugar and mix well, then add the lard and water, mixing to a soft dough. Knead lightly until smooth. Cover with plastic wrap and leave for about 30 minutes.

Thinly slice the pork and cut into small squares. Sauté the pork and onion in the oil for 1 minute; then add the sauces, sugar and sherry and sauté for 1 more minute. Mix the water and cornstarch together, pour in and sauté, stirring, until thickened. Transfer to a plate to cool.

Roll the dough out into a long sausage shape and cut into 12 pieces. Flatten each with the fingers into a circle about 4 inches across. Place a portion of filling in the center and pull the dough up around the filling, pinching it together into a point. Cut a small square of waxed paper, dip it into water and stick it over the seam.

When all buns are prepared in this way, place them paper downward in a steaming basket or on a rack. Set in the wok with the water level a good 2 inches below the rack. Cover and steam for about 12 minutes over rapidly boiling water until the buns have puffed out and are dry and springy to the touch. *Cha Siew Pow* must be served at once to be at their best.

Flatten dough, add filling and pull dough over

Wet waxed paper and place over seam

New Potatoes with Julienne Vegetables

SERVES 4–6

12 small new potatoes
1 medium carrot
1 medium zucchini
1 stick celery
1 large spring onion
2 sprigs fresh dill or fennel
¾ cup sour cream
1 tablespoon heavy cream
Salt

Set potatoes on a heatproof dish in wok

Cut vegetables into julienne strips

Thoroughly scrub the potatoes and prick in several places. Place in a heatproof dish and set on a rack in the wok. Add water to the level of the rack, cover and bring to a boil. Steam for about 8 minutes.

In the meantime, peel the vegetables and cut into julienne (matchstick) strips. Arrange over the potatoes with the herbs on top. Return to the steamer and cook for 8 more minutes, or until the potatoes and julienne vegetables are tender. Remove from the wok and drain liquid from the dish.

Mix the creams together and spoon over the vegetables or serve separately.

Zucchini or Chayote with Parsley Butter

SERVES 4–6

2 medium zucchini or chayote
Salt
Freshly ground black pepper
1½ tablespoons butter, diced
1 tablespoon parsley, finely chopped

Peel the zucchini or chayote and cut into strips. Place in a heatproof dish and sprinkle lightly with salt and pepper. Set on a rack in the wok and steam over rapidly boiling water for about 8 minutes, tightly covered.

Drain off any liquid that has accumulated in the dish; add the butter and the parsley. Return to the steamer and cook for 1 to 2 more minutes. Serve at once.

Peel chayote, if used, under water to prevent staining hands

Slice chayote or zucchini, then cut into strips

Broccoli Hollandaise

SERVES 4–6

Try this recipe also for Brussels sprouts, asparagus or small new potatoes, adjusting the cooking time accordingly.

2 large heads broccoli
2 teaspoons butter, cut
   into small dice
¾ teaspoon salt

Quick Hollandaise Sauce
¼ cup butter
6 egg yolks
1 tablespoon lemon juice
Pinch of salt

Dot butter on broccoli florets

Wash the broccoli thoroughly and cut into florets. Place in a dish with the flowers facing upward and scatter the butter pieces and salt over the top. Set on a rack in the wok, add water to the level of the rack, cover and steam for about 15 minutes or until just tender. Do not overcook.

To make the Hollandaise Sauce, melt the butter until it just begins to bubble, then remove quickly from the heat. Place the egg yolks, lemon juice and salt into a blender or food processor and blend until slightly thickened; then slowly drizzle in the butter, blending until all has been incorporated. Serve with the hot vegetables.

Little Carrot Cups

SERVES 6

1 pound carrots
1 tablespoon lemon juice
3 tablespoons butter, softened
2 eggs
¾ teaspoon salt
¼ teaspoon sugar
1½ teaspoons parsley, finely chopped, or 6 capers

Peel the carrots, slice them and cook in boiling water without salt for 12 to 15 minutes until tender.

Drain the carrots well and transfer to a blender or food processor with the remaining ingredients, except parsley or capers. Blend to a smooth purée.

Butter six small heatproof dishes or cups and sprinkle in the chopped parsley, or place a caper in the bottom of each. Pour in the carrot mixture and cover each with a piece of buttered aluminum foil.

Set on a rack in the wok and add water to just above the level of the rack. Cover and bring to a boil. Steam for about 18 minutes until set. Remove from the wok and leave to stand in the dishes for about 3 minutes before turning out to serve.

Spoon puréed carrot mixture into dishes

Place in basket, cover and steam

Steak and Kidney Pudding

SERVES 6

Pastry
¼ pound fresh suet, grated
1½ cups flour
½ cup fresh (soft) white bread crumbs
½ teaspoon salt
¾ cup water

Filling
1½ pounds stewing steaks
3 tablespoons seasoned flour
½ pound ox kidneys
1 small onion
½ cup fresh mushrooms
2 teaspoons Worcestershire sauce (optional)
2 teaspoons tomato paste, purée or powder
1¼ teaspoons salt
½ teaspoon freshly ground black pepper
¾ cup beef stock

Place the suet in a mixing bowl and sift on the flour. Add the crumbs and salt and mix thoroughly. Pour in the water and work to a soft dough. Roll out on a floured board to about ¼ inch thickness. Use about three-quarters of the dough to line a 6½-cup pudding mold, reserving the remainder for the top.

Cut the steak into cubes and place in a plastic or paper bag with the seasoned flour. Trim and cube the kidneys and add to the steak. Close the bag and shake vigorously to lightly and evenly coat the meat with the flour.

Finely chop the onion and slice the mushrooms. Place a layer of meat in the pudding mold and top with a thin layer of onion and mushrooms. Repeat layering until all the filling has been used up, ending with a layer of steak and kidney.

Mix the remaining ingredients together and pour carefully down the side of the pudding. The liquid should not be less than ¾ inch from the top. Dampen the edges of the pastry with a wet finger or a pastry brush dipped in water. Reroll the remaining pastry and cut to fit the top, set in place and pinch the edges together to seal.

Cover the top with a piece of greased waxed paper and tie securely in position with string. Cover with a large square of clean cheesecloth and tie in the same way as the paper, then pull the corners of the cloth up over the top of the pudding and tie them together.

Set the pudding on a rack in the wok, add water to halfway up the sides of the pudding mold, cover and bring to a boil. Steam gently for about 5 hours, until the pastry has expanded and is light and dry to the touch, and the meat is very tender. Remove from the wok and allow to cool for about 10 minutes before opening.

When the pudding is cut open, additional rich beef stock can be added before serving, as the gravy in the pudding will be very concentrated.

Grate the fresh suet for the pastry

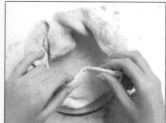
Roll pastry out and line bowl

Layer meat and vegetables in pastry-lined bowl

Top with remaining pastry; dampen edge

Baby Lamb with Herbs and Garlic

SERVES 4–6

Generous amounts of fresh herbs and garlic are used to flavor this dish, yet the result is a very subtle flavor and a delicious fragrance that complements the lamb perfectly.

2½ pounds leg of young lamb
6 to 8 sprigs fresh rosemary
6 to 8 sprigs fresh thyme
6 to 8 sprigs fresh sage or oregano
6 cloves garlic, peeled
1¼ teaspoons salt
½ teaspoon freshly ground black pepper

Trim the lamb and puncture at regular intervals with the point of a sharp knife. Insert the sprigs of herbs and the peeled whole cloves of garlic into the holes. Rub the lamb with the salt and pepper.

Place in a dish and set on a rack in the wok. Add water to the level of the rack, cover and steam over gently boiling water for about 1¾ hours, or until tender.

Drain well; carve at the table or slice the meat and arrange overlapped on a serving plate. Skim the liquid in the dish and pour into a small bowl to serve as the gravy.

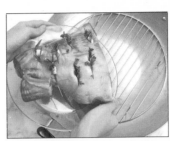

Insert herbs and garlic in cuts in lamb

Place lamb in a dish in wok on rack; add water

Pork Ribs in Black Bean and Chili Sauce

SERVES 4

Serve this salty and hot dish as an appetizer, a main course with other Chinese dishes, or with other *dim sum* dishes for a Chinese-style breakfast or brunch.

4 pork country spareribs or pork chops
2 spring onions, finely chopped
2 cloves garlic, finely chopped
2 slices fresh gingerroot, finely chopped
2 teaspoons Chinese salted black beans, chopped
1 tablespoon light soy sauce
2 teaspoons dark soy sauce
2 teaspoons sugar
1 tablespoon dry sherry
½ teaspoon sesame oil (optional)
1 fresh red chili

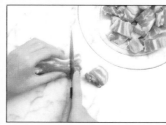

Cut spareribs into bite-sized pieces   Scatter ingredients over

Cut the pork into bite-sized pieces and place in a heatproof dish. Scatter the prepared ingredients and seasonings on top. Finely shred or chop the chili, discarding the seeds for a milder taste; sprinkle on top of the pork.

Set the dish on a rack in the wok. Add water to the level of the rack, cover and steam over gently boiling water for about 1¾ hours, until the meat is very tender.

Lion's Head Meatballs

SERVES 4

1½ pounds boneless leg of pork
1 teaspoon salt
¼ teaspoon pepper
1 tablespoon light soy sauce
2 teaspoons dry sherry
1 teaspoon sugar
¾ teaspoon sesame oil (optional)
1 (8-ounce) can water chestnuts, drained
1½ teaspoons fresh gingerroot, finely chopped
3 tablespoons spring onions, chopped
1 Chinese cabbage (bok choy) or Tientsin cabbage
1 cup chicken stock

Separate leaves and stalks of cabbage   Wrap each meatball in cabbage leaves

Cut the pork into cubes and place in a food processor fitted with the chopping blade or in a meat grinder and work to a slightly coarse paste. Mix in the seasoning ingredients.

Drain and chop the water chestnuts and mix with the pork, adding the ginger and onions. Mix well, using wet hands, then form into four large meatballs. Wash the cabbage and separate leaves and stalks. Wrap each meatball in one or two cabbage leaves. Place the stalks in the bottom of a heatproof dish and arrange the meatballs on top. Cover with cabbage leaves and pour in the stock.

Set the dish on a rack in the wok, add water to level of the rack and bring to a boil. Cover and steam for about 1 hour over rapidly boiling water.

Steamed Ham

SERVES 8

4 pounds smoked or cured ham
1 tablespoon whole cloves
1 orange
1½ tablespoons thin honey
1 tablespoon Cointreau or Grand Marnier
3 slices brown or whole-wheat bread

Remove the skin from the ham, leaving a thin layer of fat

Cut away the skin of the ham, leaving a thin layer of fat on the meat. Score through the fat in a crisscross pattern and stud with the cloves. Place the ham in a dish and set on a rack in the wok. Add water to the level of the rack, cover and steam for about 2½ hours, until the ham is tender enough for the bone to be easily pulled out. Add extra water from time to time during cooking.

Remove the ham, and discard the bone and the cloves. Grate orange rind and reserve. Squeeze the orange and mix the juice with the honey and liqueur in a small saucepan. Bring to a boil and simmer for about 2 minutes. Use a pastry brush to spread the syrup evenly over the ham. Reserve any remaining syrup to serve separately.

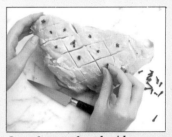

Score ham and stud with whole cloves

Toast the bread, then cut into pieces and place in a blender or food processor. Work to reasonably fine crumbs. Mix the reserved orange rind with the crumbs. Press this mixture onto the ham, coating all surfaces.

Cut into thick slices and serve warm with the syrup.

Set ham on a rack, add water and steam for about 2½ hours until tender

Oriental-style Trout with Rosemary

SERVES 2

2 fresh trout
1 teaspoon salt
2 teaspoons dry sherry
3 large fresh mushrooms
2 spring onions, shredded
5 slices fresh gingerroot, shredded
1 tablespoon light soy sauce
1½ tablespoons dry sherry
¾ teaspoon fresh rosemary, or ½ teaspoon
    dried rosemary, chopped
Pinch of freshly ground black pepper

Clean and wash the fish, leaving the heads and tails intact. Score lightly three or four times on each side. Place on an oval dish and sprinkle on the salt and 2 teaspoons of sherry. Set aside for 10 minutes.

Peel the mushrooms, remove stems and shred the caps. Arrange the shredded mushrooms, onions and ginger over the fish. Pour excess salty liquid off the fish and set the plate on a rack in the wok.

Add water to the level of the rack and bring to a boil. Pour the soy sauce and sherry over the fish and sprinkle on the rosemary and pepper. Cover tightly and steam for 9 minutes, or until the meat can be easily lifted from the bones. Serve at once on the same plate.

Score fish three to four times on each side

Fish and vegetables are set on a plate in wok

Scatter rosemary over fish and steam, covered

Steam scallops with wine and garlic

Add cooked scallops to stir-fried vegetables

Scallops in Garlic Oyster Sauce

SERVES 4–6

1½ pounds fresh scallops
1 teaspoon crushed garlic
1 tablespoon ginger wine or dry sherry
1 cup fresh bean sprouts
1 medium-sized red pepper, or chili
2 large spring onions
1½ tablespoons cooking oil

Sauce
½ cup chicken stock
2 teaspoons dark soy sauce
2 teaspoons Chinese oyster sauce
2 teaspoons cornstarch
½ teaspoon sugar

Rinse the scallops and drain. Place in a dish and add half the garlic and the wine or sherry. Mix in lightly. Set the dish on a rack in the wok and add water to the level of the rack. Cover and steam until the scallops are white.

In the meantime, rinse and drain the bean sprouts. Shred the pepper or chili and the onions, and sauté together in oil with the remaining garlic until the bean sprouts have softened.

Add the premixed sauce ingredients and bring quickly to a boil. Drain the scallops and add to the bean sprouts. Heat through in the sauce, then serve.

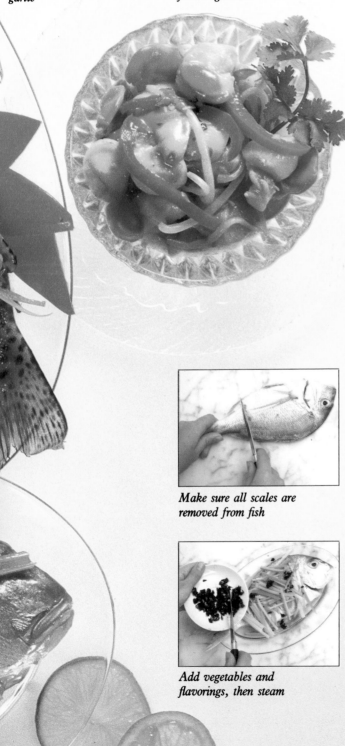

Make sure all scales are removed from fish

Add vegetables and flavorings, then steam

Fish with Black Beans and Vegetables

SERVES 4–6

2 pounds fresh whole fish (sea bass, trout)
3 to 4 slices young fresh gingerroot
⅓ stalk celery
1 small carrot
1 (8-ounce) can sliced bamboo shoots, drained
2 cloves garlic
1 tablespoon Chinese salted black beans
1 tablespoon dry sherry
2 teaspoons light soy sauce
2 teaspoons cooking oil

Clean and scale the fish. Make several cuts on each side of the fish to allow the seasonings to penetrate.

Peel and shred the ginger, celery and carrot. Shred the bamboo shoots. Finely chop the garlic and black beans.

Place the fish in a dish that will fit inside the wok. Scatter the prepared vegetables, black beans and garlic over the fish, then sprinkle on the remaining ingredients.

Set on a rack in the wok, add water to the level of the rack, and cover. Bring to a boil and steam gently for about 18 minutes. Serve.

Sweet Carrot Custards

Add milk and flavorings to carrots and cook gently

Use gloves when removing hot foods from wok

SERVES 6

1½ pounds carrots
1¾ cups milk
¼ teaspoon ground cardamom
1 teaspoon honey
1 tablespoon sugar

Custard
½ teaspoon ground cinnamon
1½ tablespoons sugar
¼ teaspoon saffron powder (optional)
2 eggs

Peel and slice the carrots. Place in a saucepan or wok with the milk, cardamom, honey and sugar. Bring to a boil, reduce heat and simmer gently until the carrot is completely tender and the milk reduced. Mash or purée in a blender or food processor until smooth.

Beat the custard ingredients together, then stir into the carrot mixture. Grease six heatproof dessert dishes and pour the mixture into them.

Cover each with a piece of buttered aluminum foil.

Set on a rack in the wok, add water to the level of the rack and cover tightly. Steam over gently boiling water for 25 minutes until softly set. Serve hot or warm in the cups with whipped cream and toasted flaked almonds. Remember to use gloves when removing dishes from wok.

Little Ginger Puddings

SERVES 6

1½ cups self-rising flour
⅓ cup butter
⅓ cup sugar
2½ tablespoons chopped ginger preserved in syrup
2 eggs, beaten
3½ tablespoons lukewarm milk
3½ tablespoons syrup from preserved ginger
Whipped cream or custard

Sift the flour onto a piece of paper. Cream the butter and sugar together, then add the ginger and beat well. Add the eggs, mixing thoroughly, then the sifted flour. Lastly, stir in just enough of the milk to make a mixture of soft dropping consistency.

Pour a little of the ginger syrup into the bottom of each of six buttered, single-serving, pudding molds or other heatproof dishes. Divide the batter among the dishes and cover each with a piece of buttered aluminum foil.

Set on a rack in the wok and add water to just above the rack. Cover and steam for about 1 hour, or until the puddings feel firm and springy to the touch and have loosened from the sides of the dishes. Turn out into dessert dishes and serve hot with whipped cream or custard.

Drained canned mandarin segments, heated in additional ginger syrup with a touch of slivered ginger, transforms this simple steamed pudding into a memorable dessert.

Pour a little ginger syrup into each mold

Crème Caramel

SERVES 6

2½ cups milk
½ cup sugar
3 eggs
1 egg yolk
Pinch of salt
¾ teaspoon vanilla
  extract

Caramel
½ cup sugar
1 tablespoon water

Heat the milk and sugar together, stirring until sugar dissolves and the milk is just warm. Remove from the heat. Beat the eggs and yolk lightly together and add the salt. Stir into the milk, and then beat with an electric or hand mixer for about 3 minutes. Add the vanilla, then set aside.

Place the caramel ingredients in a saucepan. Cook over moderate heat, stirring occasionally until the sugar is dissolved; then allow the syrup to bubble gently until it turns a light golden color. Pour into a heatproof dish that wil hold about 3½ cups and swirl so that the toffee coats the bottom of the dish and runs halfway up the sides.

Pour in the custard, cover with a piece of aluminum foil pierced in several places, then set on a rack in the wok. Cover and steam over gently boiling water for about 25 minutes, or until the custard is set. Turn out onto a serving dish and chill thoroughly before serving with whipped cream.

If preferred, the custards can be cooked in smaller individual serving dishes. These will require only about 18 minutes cooking time, but otherwise should be prepared in the same way as the larger custard.

Swirl caramel in dish to coat evenly

Pierce foil to allow steam to escape

Lemon Egg Custard

SERVES 6

6 whole eggs
3 egg whites
1½ cups milk
2 tablespoons thin honey
2 teaspoons cornstarch
¾ teaspoon lemon rind, grated

Topping
1 lemon
3 tablespoons sugar
½ cup water

Beat the eggs and egg whites together. Add the milk, honey and cornstarch and beat until smooth. Stir in the lemon rind.

Pour the mixture into six oiled, heatproof dishes. Cover with aluminum foil and set on a rack in the steamer. Add water to just below the rack, cover and steam over gently boiling water for about 15 minutes, until the custards are set.

In the meantime, peel the lemon and very finely shred the lemon rind after scraping away the pith. Place in a saucepan with the sugar and water and bring to a slow boil. Stir until the sugar has dissolved, then simmer gently until the syrup turns a light golden color and is slightly sticky. Add about 1 tablespoon of lemon juice and stir on moderate heat until any toffee lumps that form have dissolved. Pour a little over each custard and serve hot.

If preferred, omit the lemon juice from the toffee. Chill the custards, top with the toffee and chill again until hard. Serve cold with whipped cream.

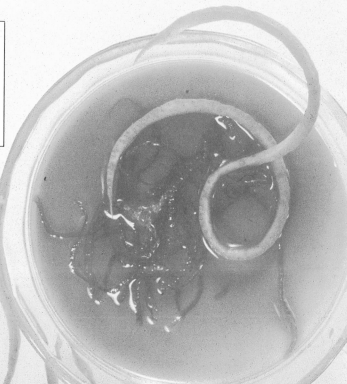

Pour custard into heatproof bowls

Scrape white pith away from lemon rind, then shred

Add lemon juice to the sugar syrup

Babas au Kirsch

MAKES 10

2 cups flour
1 package dried yeast
  granules
½ cup lukewarm milk
3 tablespoons sugar
4 egg yolks
Grated rind of ½ lemon
½ cup butter (preferably
  clarified)
1 pint fresh strawberries
Whipped cream
Kirsch

Syrup
2¼ cups sugar
2 cups water
3 tablespoons Kirsch

Add spongy yeast mixture to flour

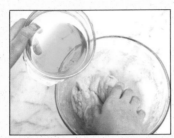

Slowly work butter into the dough

Press dough gently into greased molds

Sift the flour into a mixing bowl and set in a warm place.

Sprinkle the yeast over 3 tablespoons of the milk, whisk with a fork, and leave for about 12 minutes until dissolved and beginning to bubble. Then add 1 teaspoon of the sugar and 1 tablespoon of the flour, mix in well, and leave until the mixture becomes spongy.

Beat the remaining sugar, the egg yolks and lemon rind together and set aside.

Melt the butter gently in a small saucepan, then remove from the heat and allow to settle. Strain the butter, leaving the white residue behind. If using clarified butter, simply melt gently and set aside.

Make a well in the flour, and pour in the yeast and egg mixtures. Mix in lightly, then gradually add the remaining milk, working to a soft dough. Use your hands to knead the dough in the bowl. Slowly add the butter, kneading and folding the dough until all the butter is incorporated and the dough is soft, shiny and smooth. When ready, it should no longer stick to the fingers. Cover and leave in a warm place until doubled in volume.

Select 10 small baba molds, brioche tins or heatproof dishes, and brush with melted butter. Divide the dough into 10 equal portions and press gently into the molds. Set aside, uncovered, until well risen.

Hull the strawberries, reserving 10 for decoration. Slice the remainder, then chill.

Pour the sugar and water for the syrup into a saucepan and stir slowly until the sugar has dissolved; then leave to boil for about 6 minutes until just slightly sticky. Remove from the heat and leave to cool, then add the Kirsch.

Prepare the whipped cream and flavor it with Kirsch. Set aside.

Place the *babas* on a rack in the wok, add water to the level of the rack and cover with the lid. Bring to a boil and steam over rapidly boiling water for 15 to 18 minutes, until the cakes feel dry and springy.

Remove from the wok and turn them onto a cake rack to cool. Puncture all over with a sharp skewer. When cooled, place the *babas* in a dish and pour on the syrup. Refrigerate until quite cold.

To assemble, transfer the *babas* to individual dessert dishes. Top with the strawberries, placing a whole strawberry in the center, then surround with the whipped cream.

Traditional Plum Pudding

SERVES 8–12

1 box raisins
1 box white raisins
1 box currants
1 cup suet, grated
2 cups fresh brown
  bread crumbs
2 tablespoons candied
  peel
2 tablespoons slivered
  almonds
1 cooking apple, peeled
  and sliced
2¼ cups brown sugar
1 teaspoon salt
2 teaspoons allspice
1 teaspoon ground
  cinnamon
¼ teaspoon grated
  nutmeg
2 eggs, well beaten
1 lemon
1 orange
1½ tablespoons brandy
  or rum
1 cup flour

Rum Butter
2¼ cups dark brown
  sugar
¼ cup butter (preferably
  unsalted)
3 tablespoons dark rum
Nutmeg

Add suet, crumbs and flavorings to fruit

Turn mixture into a greased pudding mold

Knot corners of prepared pudding cloth together

Wash the dried fruits and dry thoroughly. Place in a mixing bowl and add the suet, crumbs, peel, almonds, apple and sugar and mix thoroughly. Add the salt, spices and eggs and mix well. Grate the rind of the lemon and orange, then squeeze the juice. Add to the mixture with the remaining ingredients and mix thoroughly.

Pour the mixture into a well-greased 6½-cup pudding mold. Cover with a piece of greased mold waxed paper, tied securely in place with string. Then cover with a scalded and floured cheesecloth and tie in place.

Set the dish on a rack in the wok, add water to halfway up the sides of the dish, and bring to a boil. Cover and steam over gently boiling water for 6 to 7 hours. Add more water from time to time during cooking.

Lift out and leave to cool for a few minutes, then remove the cheesecloth. Uncover the pudding and turn out onto a serving plate. Cut into wedges and serve hot with custard, Rum Butter or whipped cream. The pudding may be flamed with warmed liquor before serving.

To make the Rum Butter, beat the sugar and butter together until soft and light, then add the rum and nutmeg. Chill until firm before serving. Rum Butter can be kept for several weeks in the refrigerator.

Cooked plum puddings can be kept for several months before use. Wrap in several layers of aluminum foil and store in a cool cupboard. Steam for about 1½ hours before serving; the longer you steam it, the darker it becomes.

Orange Pudding

SERVES 6–8

1½ cups self-rising flour
½ cup butter
⅓ cup sugar
2 eggs, beaten
3 tablespoons orange jam/marmalade
1 teaspoon orange rind, grated
3 tablespoons warm milk

Orange Custard
2 cups orange juice, freshly squeezed
½ teaspoon orange rind, grated
4 egg yolks
¼ cup sugar
2 teaspoons cornstarch
1 tablespoon cold water

Sift the flour onto a plate. Cream the butter and sugar together until light and creamy. Add the beaten eggs and the jam or marmalade and mix well. Add the rind. Fold in the sifted flour and mix thoroughly. Add just enough warm milk to make a soft dropping consistency.

Grease a 2-pint pudding mold or eight custard cups and pour in the mixture. Cover with a piece of greased waxed paper and set on a rack in the wok.

Add water to just above the rack, cover and steam over gently boiling water for about 1¼ hours for a large pudding or 30 minutes for small puddings.

When the pudding is done, it will begin to come away from the sides of the mold. Let it stand for about 5 minutes, then turn out onto a serving plate. Serve hot with Orange Custard, or with cream and marmalade topping—marmalade heated with butter until it just reaches boiling point.

To make the Orange Custard, place the orange juice in a saucepan and heat until almost boiling. Then remove from the heat and leave to cool.

Beat the orange rind, egg yolks and sugar together until creamy. Mix the cornstarch and cold water together, then beat into the egg mixture. Stand the dish on a rack in the wok with water around the bottom of the dish barely simmering. Gradually add the orange juice to the egg mixture, beating briskly until the custard is thick enough to coat the back of a spoon. Serve hot with the Orange Pudding.

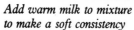

Add warm milk to mixture to make a soft consistency

Turn into custard cups and steam, covered with foil

Braising

The Chinese never considered the wok as an important pan for braising and stewing. This was usually done in a deep pottery pot over a small clay charcoal-burning stove.

But its possibilities as a stewpan should not be overlooked. To begin with, it is larger than most pans in the domestic kitchen, making it invaluable for those times when you're faced with the task of cooking for a crowd. It can be used to cook a large whole joint—say, a leg of lamb or pork, or even a whole turkey—utilizing its domed lid to create extra capacity. It handles the preliminary browning/searing that should be done before meat begins to stew with ease and efficiency.

Its success as a braising/stewing pan, however, depends primarily on the flexibility of the heat source beneath it. In this instance, gas, which is so eminently suitable for quick stir-frying, often cannot be regulated to offer the low-simmering temperatures required for braising. If your gas stove does not have a very low-regulating ring, the problem can be overcome by placing the wok on a *wok stand* to raise it slightly above the gas ring. This introduces a cooling air buffer between the wok and its heat source. Some electric stoves may also require a wok stand to modify the cooking temperature.

Wok stands are readily available where woks and other Chinese cooking equipment are sold. They are particularly necessary if you intend to use your wok as a deep-fryer as well, because it is essential to have a steady base on which to rest a hot wok filled with cooking oil after it has been used.

Stainless steel and aluminum woks are perhaps more suited to braising than iron or steel woks. I have noticed on occasion that my braised dishes have acquired a hint of a metallic taste when cooked in my standard wok, particularly dishes with acidic sauces such as those cooked with wine or citrus juices. I have found, in fact, that an electric wok is very well suited to braising. The nonstick coating on the inside prevents sticking as well as eliminating the possibility of contamination of flavors.

Braising is simple. The meat should be browned and sealed before stewing to prevent it drying out and shrinking, thus becoming tough, and also to lend color to both the meat and the resultant sauce.

Have the wok on fairly high heat, add cooking oil, fat or butter, and then brown the meat, several pieces at a time, turning to ensure that all surfaces are evenly browned. Do not crowd the wok at this stage or the meat will not brown sufficiently. Remove each piece when done, and brown the remainder in batches, then return the meat to the pan and add the remaining ingredients. Bring the liquid just to a boil, then reduce the heat and simmer for the required cooking time. The fragments of meat that adhere to the pan during browning will flake off during cooking to add flavor and color to the sauce.

When braising poultry, the wings and breasts may be added to the pan after the remainder has been partially cooked, to prevent them overcooking.

Liquids added to meat for stewing/braising should be lukewarm or even hot—never ice cold as this can cause the meat to toughen. If additional liquid is to be added to the dish during cooking, this must always be warm or hot.

Celery in Mustard Sauce

SERVES 4–6

4 stalks fresh celery
3 tablespoons butter
¾ cup chicken stock
3 tablespoons milk
1½ teaspoons prepared English mustard
3 teaspoons flour
1 egg yolk
3 tablespoons heavy cream
Salt and black pepper

Wash the celery and cut into 4-inch pieces. Sauté in 2 tablespoons of the butter until it begins to soften (about 3 minutes). Add the chicken stock, milk and mustard. Cover and simmer gently for about 20 minutes.

Remove the celery to a serving plate. Mix the flour and remaining butter together and stir into the sauce to thicken. Beat the egg yolk and cream together lightly and add to the sauce off the heat. Beat briskly until smooth and thick. Season to taste and pour over the celery. Serve at once.

Wash celery and cut into 4-inch pieces

Add butter and flour to sauce

Braised Red Cabbage

SERVES 4

1 head red cabbage
1 tablespoon butter
1 medium onion, finely chopped
¼ cup sugar
1 cooking apple, sliced
1 tablespoon white vinegar
3 tablespoons water
1 teaspoon salt
⅓ teaspoon caraway seeds

Shred the cabbage, discarding the outer leaves and core. Heat the butter in the wok and sauté the onion until transparent. Add the sugar, apple, vinegar and water and bring to a boil. Add the cabbage, cover the wok and braise gently for about 1 hour.

Season with the salt and caraway seeds about 15 minutes before the cabbage is ready.

Discard core and outer leaves and shred cabbage

Add cabbage to wok and braise until cooked

Leeks in Tomato and Parsley Sauce

SERVES 4–6

6 fresh leeks
1 medium onion, sliced
3 tablespoons olive oil
1 large tomato, chopped
1 tablespoon tomato paste
**   or purée**
½ cup parsley, chopped
¾ cup water
Salt and black pepper
Lemon juice

Remove the coarse outer leaves from the leeks and trim off the root, cutting from two sides to form a point. Split the white parts down the center. This preparation makes it easier to clean the leeks. Wash thoroughly in cold water and drain.

Sauté the onion in the oil until transparent. Then add the tomato and sauté until softened. Stir in the tomato paste and half the parsley; add the water. Bring to a boil, cover the wok and simmer for 7 to 8 minutes.

Add the leeks, cover again and braise gently until the leeks are tender (about 20 minutes). Add salt, pepper and lemon juice to taste; then stir in the remaining parsley. Serve hot or well chilled.

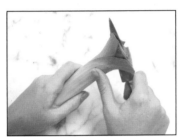
Split leeks down center for washing

Wash under running cold water to remove all grit

Add leeks to tomato mixture, then braise

Boeuf Bourguignon

SERVES 4–6

1½ pounds good stewing steak
1½ cups good red wine
1 bouquet garni (bunch of fresh herbs)
4 black peppercorns
¼ pound salt pork or bacon
12 small (pickling) onions
2 tablespoons lard
1 tablespoon flour
⅓ teaspoon grated nutmeg
Salt and black pepper

Trim the steak and cut into small cubes. Place in a dish with the wine, herbs and peppercorns, cover with plastic wrap and leave for about 5 hours.

Cut the pork or bacon into small cubes. Peel the onions. Heat the lard in the wok and fry the pork and onions until the pork is quite crisp and the onions browned. Remove and set aside.

Drain the meat, reserving the marinade, and fry in the remaining fat until evenly browned. Cook in two or three batches to ensure meat is sealed.

Sprinkle on the flour and leave to brown slightly, then return all the meat, the pork and onions to the wok; add the nutmeg and a dash of salt and pepper. Pour in the reserved marinade and bring to a boil. Cover tightly and simmer gently for about 2 hours on moderate to low heat. Shake the wok from time to time to turn the meat. If preferred, the onions can be added in the last 30 minutes of cooking to prevent them overcooking.

Greek-style Beef

Sofrito

SERVES 6

2½ pounds blade or chuck steak
1 cup flour
1½ teaspoons salt
½ teaspoon freshly ground black pepper
3 tablespoons olive oil
1 tablespoon butter
2 to 4 cloves garlic, crushed
3 tablespoons wine vinegar
3 tablespoons red wine
1 teaspoon sugar
2 tablespoons parsley, chopped
1 cup water or beef stock

Cut the meat into cubes. Mix the flour, salt and pepper together in a plastic or paper bag and add the meat. Shake briskly until the meat is evenly coated, then transfer to a colander and shake off any excess flour.

Marinate meat in wine and herbs for 5 hours

Fry salt pork and peeled onions until crisp

Braise gently, stirring occasionally

Heat the olive oil and butter in the wok, and brown the meat in several batches until evenly browned. Add the garlic and cook briefly. Return all the meat, add the vinegar and wine, bring almost to a boil, then simmer for 3 minutes. Add the sugar, parsley and water; cover the wok and simmer gently for about 1¼ hours, until the meat is completely tender and will cut with a fork.

Serve with mashed potatoes or boiled pasta and sautéed spinach or other green vegetables.

Goulash

SERVES 4

1¼ pounds veal steak
3 tablespoons olive oil or cooking oil
1 medium onion, finely chopped
¾ teaspoon sweet paprika
Salt
½ cup water
½ cup sour cream

Cut the veal into small cubes and sauté in two or three batches in the oil until evenly browned. Remove and keep warm.

Add the onion and fry until lightly browned and softened. Return the meat and add the paprika and salt. Pour in the water, cover the wok and braise gently for about 1½ hours until the meat is completely tender.

Add a little hot water from time to time during cooking to prevent the dish drying up and sticking to the pan. Just before serving, stir in the sour cream and heat through.

Shake cubed meat in a bag to coat with flour

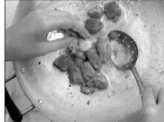
Brown meat in several batches

Add paprika and salt to browned veal and onion in wok

Add sour cream to goulash just before serving and heat through

Lamb Korma

SERVES 4

2 pounds shoulder or leg lamb
2 medium onions
3 tablespoons clarified butter
1 tablespoon ground coriander
1½ teaspoons ground cumin
½ teaspoon chili powder
2 to 3 cloves garlic, chopped
1½ teaspoons fresh gingerroot, grated
3 tablespoons ground almonds
¾ cup natural yogurt
1 teaspoon salt
¼ teaspoon freshly ground black pepper

Cut the lamb into cubes, discarding bones and fat. Thinly slice
1 onion and grate or chop the other.

Fry the lamb in the butter until evenly browned. Add the
onions and fry until these are browned. Then add the spices,
garlic and ginger, and fry briefly. Add the ground almonds and
the yogurt and braise gently until the liquid has been absorbed
(about 25 minutes).

Add salt and pepper and enough water to just cover the
meat. Cover and braise gently until the meat is very tender
(about 45 minutes). Shake the wok occasionally to turn the
meat, but keep the lid on
throughout the cooking.
Serve with saffron rice
and a spicy chutney.

Cut lamb into cubes,
discarding bones and fat

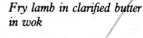
Fry lamb in clarified butter
in wok

Add yogurt to curry
mixture and braise gently

Lamb Rolls Stuffed with Apple and Coriander

SERVES 4

This innovative use of lamb loin cutlets can be served as a main course, or sliced and served hot or cold as an appetizer.

2 loins (racks) of lamb, each of 6 cutlets
¾ cooking apple
½ tablespoon ground coriander
½ cup seasoned flour
1 tablespoon cooking oil
3 tablespoons butter
1¼ cups apple juice or cider
2 teaspoons parsley, chopped

Bone the loins and trim away excess fat. Peel, core and slice the apple. Season the inside of the loins with the coriander and plenty of salt and pepper. Place the sliced apple along the center of each. Roll up the lamb with the meaty "eye" section inside. Tie securely with clean string. Roll in seasoned flour, coating lightly.

Heat the oil and butter together in the wok and sauté the lamb rolls until well and evenly browned. Pour off the fat and add the apple juice. Bring just to a boil, then reduce the heat; cover and braise for about 30 minutes until the lamb is just cooked through and the juice reduced to a tangy dark glaze on the meat. Shake the pan from time to time during cooking to turn the rolls to ensure that they are evenly cooked and glazed.

Transfer to a serving plate after cutting each roll in half through the center. Pour on any remaining glaze and garnish with the chopped parsley.

Trim all fat away from boned loins of lamb

Place apple slices in the seasoned lamb

Roll up and tie with string

Add apple juice to the browned meat and braise

Lebanese Orange Duck

SERVES 6–8

4½ pounds duck
1 large onion, chopped
3½ tablespoons butter
3 large oranges
½ lemon
Salt and black pepper
1 tablespoon flour
1 tablespoon toasted almonds

Brown duck on all sides, turning with two wooden spoons to protect skin

Pour in orange and lemon juice and braise the duck until tender

Duck may be served whole or cut into serving pieces

Clean and dress the duck. Sauté the onion in the butter until lightly browned. Push to one side of the pan and put in the duck. Brown gently all over, turning it with two wooden spoons to avoid breaking the skin. Pour off the fat.

Squeeze the juice from 2 oranges and the lemon and pour over the duck. Add salt and pepper, cover the wok and braise gently for about 1½ hours until completely tender. The pan juices should be reduced to a rich dark glaze. Turn the duck several times to ensure even cooking. When done, remove the duck from the wok.

Sprinkle the flour into the wok and add the juice of the remaining orange. Bring to a boil, stirring, then cook until the sauce is thick. If the duck is a fat one, pour off most of the fat that will have accumulated in the wok before making the sauce. Serve the duck on a platter garnished with orange slices and parsley and carve at the table. Alternatively, cut the duck into 6 to 8 pieces and arrange on a serving dish garnished with toasted almonds.

Coq au Vin

SERVES 6

3 pounds roasting
   chicken
2 slices bacon
12 small (pickling) onions
24 small fresh mushrooms
2 tablespoons butter
2 tablespoons olive oil
   or cooking oil
Salt and black pepper
½ cup flour
2 cloves garlic, chopped
3 tablespoons brandy
2 cups good red wine
1 cup chicken stock
2 sprigs parsley
⅓ teaspoon dried thyme
2 bay leaves
1 tablespoon flour
½ teaspoon sugar
3 tablespoons parsley, chopped

Wash the chicken and wipe dry. Cut into six pieces: two leg and thigh portions, two wing and breast portions and two lower breast sections. Dice the bacon. Peel the onions. Trim the mushrooms.

Heat the butter and oil together in the wok. Add the bacon; sauté until beginning to crisp, then remove. Add the onions and cook until lightly browned; add the mushrooms and cook until beginning to soften. Remove.

Season the chicken pieces with salt and pepper, then coat lightly with ½ cup flour. Cook two pieces at a time, until evenly browned.

When all are done, return the chicken, bacon and vegetables to the wok and add the garlic. Cover and braise gently for about 15 minutes.

Remove the chicken and other ingredients from the wok and skim off the fat. Warm the brandy in a ladle and ignite it, pour into the wok and extinguish with the wine and stock. Bring to a boil; add the herbs, flour, sugar and a little extra butter; and whisk vigorously until smooth. Boil until the sauce is reduced by one-third.

Return the chicken and other ingredients. Cover the wok and braise for about 45 minutes until the chicken is tender. The sauce should be sufficiently thick by this time.

Stir in the chopped parsley, check the seasonings and serve.

Cut chicken into six pieces, then coat with flour

Add mushrooms to browned onions in wok

Remove chicken from wok

Outdoor Cooking

If you've ever taken good saucepans, kettle and frying pan on a camping spree, they've probably come back blackened with smoke, and with handles badly charred. This needn't happen if you take an inexpensive rolled-steel wok instead. It functions as frying pan, stewpot, oven and kettle all in one. And the only other pieces of equipment necessary to pack are its lid, a metal rack to use if you plan to do a little steaming or smoking, a good-sized ladle and the "charn" spatula.

A camp-fire wok begins its day as a kettle to boil water for a mug of coffee or pot of tea, and there's plenty of hot water left over for a shave or to do the previous night's dishes. A rinse and rub-out with a paper towel and it's ready for omelettes, or eggs and bacon, or to receive those promised freshly caught fish.

Then throughout the day, it remains busy—frying up noodles, stewing meat and vegetables, poaching, steaming, boiling—with no more care needed than a brisk scrub at the nearest source of clean water. And last thing at night after the meal is finished and the campsite put in order, you can relax around the fading fire to mull a bottle of red wine, adding cloves, orange zest, cinnamon and a good big dash of brandy.

When the wok is used at the campsite, it sits directly in a bed of glowing coals, or is supported over the fire on a ring of rocks or wood blocks. Its looped metal handles cannot be damaged through too-close contact with the fire; and its bottom, though soon pitch-black, will be unmarked.

You can also use the wok when you cook outdoors at home. The wok for outdoor cooking is practical and will soon become indispensable.

Spanish Omelette

SERVES 4

2 large potatoes
2 medium onions
1 red or green pepper
3 tablespoons olive oil
1 tablespoon butter
2 teaspoons parsley*, finely chopped
½ teaspoon fresh oregano or sage*, chopped
¾ teaspoon salt
Pinch of freshly ground black pepper
3 eggs, beaten

Tomato Sauce
1 medium onion, finely chopped
1 clove garlic, chopped
3 tablespoons celery, finely chopped
1½ tablespoons butter
3 tablespoons mushrooms, finely chopped
2 medium tomatoes, peeled and chopped
¾ teaspoon salt
Large pinch of freshly ground black pepper
1 teaspoon sugar
½ cup chicken stock or water

Peel the potatoes and onions and cut into small dice.
Remove stem, seed pod and inner ribs from the pepper
and cut into small squares or narrow strips.

Heat the oil and butter in the wok and put in the
vegetables. Sauté gently, covered, for about 15 minutes until
the potatoes are just tender. Shake the pan from time to time
to turn the vegetables, and stir if needed to prevent sticking.

Add the herbs, salt and pepper, and mix in lightly.
Pour on the beaten eggs and leave to cook very gently until
firm. Serve immediately with fresh Tomato Sauce.

To make Tomato Sauce, place the onion, garlic and
celery in a saucepan or wok with the butter; cover and cook
gently for about 7 minutes. Add the mushrooms and cook for
2 to 3 more minutes. Add the chopped tomato, stir;
then season with the salt, pepper and sugar and cook for
3 to 4 minutes. Add the stock or water and simmer gently
for about 15 minutes, until the sauce is thick. It may be passed
through a sieve to produce a smooth sauce, if preferred.

* If fresh herbs are unavailable, use half quantities of dried herbs.

Sauté vegetables until tender

Add herbs and seasonings to
vegetables

Pour in beaten eggs and cook
gently

Paella

SERVES 6

2½ cups raw long-grain rice
½ cup olive oil
⅓ teaspoon saffron powder
1½ teaspoons salt
3 Chorizo sausages, sliced
2 large slices streaky bacon, or 2 slices
    raw smoked ham, diced
1 medium onion, chopped
½ pound boneless chicken
½ pound fish fillets
6 large uncooked shrimp, in the shell
12 black olives, pitted
6½ cups water or chicken stock
1 green pepper
1 red pepper
¼ cup frozen green peas, thawed
12 clams or mussels, in the shell
1 small crab

Place the rice in the wok with the olive oil, saffron and salt and sauté until the rice turns a light golden brown. Add the sliced Chorizo sausage, diced bacon or ham and the onion and continue to sauté, stirring continually, until the bacon begins to crisp and the onion is lightly browned.

Cut the chicken and fish into cubes. Add to the wok with the shrimp, washed but not shelled, and the olives. Add the water or chicken stock and bring briskly to a boil, stirring; reduce the heat, cover the wok and simmer very gently.

Remove stems, seed pods and inner ribs from the peppers and cut them into small squares. Add to the rice, together with the peas, scrubbed clams or mussels and the crab, which has been cut into large pieces and inedible parts removed. Cover the wok and leave to simmer for 8 to 10 minutes more, until the rice and all ingredients are tender.

Stir so that the meat and vegetables are evenly distributed in the rice. Serve in large bowls.

Add sausage, bacon and onion to rice in wok

Add chicken, fish, shrimp and olives

Pour in water or chicken stock and simmer.

Add mussels and crab to other ingredients in wok

Shrimp Cooked in Salt

SERVES 6 AS AN APPETIZER OR MAIN COURSE

6 very large raw shrimp, in their shells
2 pounds sea salt

Sauce
3 tablespoons light soy sauce
1 fresh red chili, chopped
1 tablespoon cooking oil

Trim the shrimp legs. Cut down the center of their backs through the shells and pull away the intestinal veins.

Line the wok with a piece of aluminum foil and put in the salt. Cover the wok and heat until the salt is quite hot to the touch. Remove half the salt, smooth flat and place the shrimp on the remaining salt. Cover with the salt that was removed. Cover the wok and cook over moderate heat for about 12 minutes. The cooked meat should be firm and white. Do not overcook.

Mix the sauce ingredients together and pour into small dishes. Brush the salt off the shrimp. Serve with lemon wedges and the sauce.

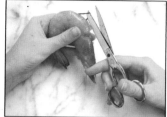

Cut shrimp through the center of the back shell and remove vein

Heat salt in foil-lined wok, add shrimp and cover with remaining salt

Catch of the Day

SERVES 2

2 freshly caught fish
3 tablespoons flour
Salt and black pepper
Juice of ½ lemon
¼ cup butter
Parsley

Clean and scale the fish and wash well; dry with a paper towel. Mix the flour, salt and pepper together. Score each side of the fish lightly in several places and sprinkle on a little lemon juice. Coat lightly with the seasoned flour.

Melt the butter in the wok until it begins to foam. Put in the fish and fry on moderate heat on each side for about 3 minutes, turning carefully. Sprinkle with the remaining lemon juice, garnish with parsley, and serve at once.

Score fish and sprinkle with lemon juice

Coat lightly with seasoned flour

Quick Sourdough Bread

SERVES 6

**2½ cups white or whole-wheat self-rising
  flour**
**2 cups buttermilk, or a mixture of water
  and plain yogurt**
1 teaspoon salt
1 cup raisins, optional

Sift the flour into a mixing bowl and add the buttermilk (or
yogurt and water) and the salt. Mix thoroughly, then add the
raisins, if used, and mix in.

Thickly butter a large sheet of aluminum foil, then cut
another piece of foil the same size. Place the dough in the
center of the buttered foil and seal, allowing room for
expansion. Wrap this in the unbuttered foil.

Place a metal rack in the wok and set the wok over gently
glowing coals. Place the parcel on the rack, cover the wok and
cook gently for about 30 minutes; then turn and cook for 30
minutes more, or until the bread is cooked through, dry and
springy to the touch. Serve with plenty of butter.

*Turn dough onto a sheet of
thickly buttered foil*

*Seal edges allowing room for
expansion*

German Apple Pancake
Apfelpfannkuchen

SERVES 4–6

Despite its lengthy name, this pan-cooked apple cake/pancake is quick and easy to make.

2 large green (cooking) apples
¼ cup raisins
1 tablespoon sugar
1 teaspoon ground cinnamon
¼ cup butter
1 tablespoon brandy (optional)
3 eggs
¼ cup flour
¼ cup milk
1 tablespoon sugar
Pinch of salt
2 teaspoons brown sugar (optional)

Peel, core and slice the apples. Place in the wok with the raisins, sugar, cinnamon and half the butter. Cover and cook very gently for about 7 minutes until the apple is tender. Increase the heat, add the brandy if used, and cook for 1 more minute. Transfer to a plate and rinse out the wok.

Beat the eggs with the flour and milk for 2 minutes, then add the sugar and salt and beat again until dissolved.

Melt the remaining butter in the wok and pour in the batter. Cover and cook very gently for 10 minutes.

Spread the apples over the top of the pancake, cover the wok again and cook for 12 to 15 minutes, until the pancake is firm and slightly puffed. Do not allow it to cook too quickly. Slide the pancake onto a plate and sprinkle on the brown sugar, if used. Serve at once. Decorate with whipped cream and cinnamon, if desired.

Cook apples in covered wok until tender

Spread apples over cooked batter

Pancakes with Maple Syrup

SERVES 4

Pancakes never taste better than when eaten outdoors. An iron wok nestled into coals should cook them perfectly.

2½ cups whole-wheat or white self-rising flour
¼ cup sugar
Small pinch of salt
3 medium eggs, beaten
1¼ cups milk
1 cup maple syrup or thin honey
Butter, preferably unsalted

Sift the flour into a mixing bowl and add the sugar and salt. Stir in the eggs and milk and beat for 2 minutes, then set aside for about 10 minutes to allow the flour to soften and the rising agents to activate.

Warm the syrup or honey in a small saucepan on the edge of the fire. Beat the butter with a fork until light and fluffy. Set aside.

Vigorously rub the interior of the wok with an oiled paper towel until it appears smooth and has a dull shine.

Place the wok on the coals and heat to moderate. Pour in a large spoonful of the batter and cook until the entire surface is covered with bubbles; then turn the pancake and cook the other side until it is golden.

Serve at once, or keep warm while the remaining pancakes are cooked. Spread with the butter and pour on the syrup before serving.

Stir eggs and milk into flour to make a batter

Cook each pancake until golden on both sides

Mulled Red Wine

SERVES 4–6

1 bottle red wine
1 stick cinnamon
3 cloves
2 tablespoons sugar
1 cup brandy
Orange rind

Pour the wine into the wok and add the cinnamon and cloves. Heat gently. Mix the sugar and brandy together, stirring until the sugar dissolves. Pour into a metal ladle. Hold the orange rind above the wok with long-handled tongs. Ignite the brandy, then slowly pour it down the orange rind so that it flows into the wine. Allow to heat briefly, then ladle into mugs or stem glasses wrapped in napkins.

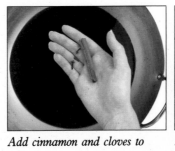
Add cinnamon and cloves to wine

Hold orange rind above wok and pour over brandy

Smoked Dishes

In the context of this collection of recipes, smoked foods are those that are smoke-cooked, not smoke-cured. The latter are foods, most commonly beef and fish, that have been subjected to a cool, smoky, enclosed atmosphere for a period of time (days or even weeks) to both dry-preserve and flavor them.

Smoke-cooking uses the heat generated from the cooking source to cook the food by indirect means, while simultaneously suffusing it with a strongly aromatic smoke. This smoky flavor thoroughly permeates the food, giving it a fragrance and taste characteristic of the smoking ingredients used, these being predominantly naturally aromatic woods in the form of chips or shavings.

Hickory wood chips are a popular smoking fuel and are now available in many stores. You can also use the smoke-fuel favored by Chinese cooks for centuries: green or black tea leaves, dried orange or tangerine peel and sugar. They also use the highly aromatic camphor wood for smoking meats, particularly duck.

Not every type of fragrant wood can be used successfully for smoking. Pine and other resinous softwoods should not be used as they will create an unpleasant flavor that would ruin the food. But oak, poplar, fruit woods such as apple and cherry, certain types of mimosa and, of course, hickory and camphor can be used.

Fresh herbs also make aromatic smoke-fuel. Branches or large sprigs of fresh rosemary, bay or thyme will give the meat an elusive flavor.

Smoke-cooking in a wok is simple. A heavy iron wok makes the ideal smoke-cooker. It should remain unaffected through exposure to direct heat, where a cooking pot of less sturdy construction might buckle or burn. If an aluminum, stainless steel, nonstick-coated or electric wok is to be used, test it cautiously on moderate temperatures to avoid damage.

The wok should preferably be used outdoors, either on a portable gas or electric ring, or over a charcoal or wood fire, as the smoke can be quite pervasive and acrid.

A double thickness of aluminum foil in the bottom of the wok will prevent burnt chips sticking to the pan and possibly spoiling the surface. The chips are placed directly on the foil, and a metal rack of open construction is placed over the chips, allowing space for the smoke to circulate. The food to be smoked is placed directly on the rack, which should be rubbed with oil to prevent sticking. Cuts of meat should be first sealed by quickly searing (browning) in the wok with a little cooking oil or beef drippings. This prevents the natural moisture of the meat being drawn out during the cooking/smoking process.

Meats, fish and poultry can be completely dry smoke-cooked. That is, they simply sit on the rack and cook slowly in the dry smoky heat generated below. Or they can be cooked in a combination of steam and smoke, by adding water to the smoke-fuel below the rack. The water will first create steam and then, as it evaporates, the smoke-fuel will dry out and eventually begin to smoke, to complete the cooking cycle with dry smoke heat. This method is particularly effective for delicate and lean meats such as chicken or quail, which may become dried out by smoke-cooking alone.

Chinese Smoked Chicken

SERVES 4

2½ pounds chicken
3 tablespoons Chinese black tea leaves
½ dried orange rind
1 tablespoon sugar

Wash the chicken and wipe dry. Set on a rack in the wok and add water to below the level of the rack. Cover and steam for about 45 minutes, turning twice.

Remove the chicken and the rack, and drain off the remaining water. Line the wok with a double thickness of aluminum foil and add the remaining ingredients.

Set over high heat until they begin to smoke. Then return the chicken to the rack, cover the wok and smoke over moderate heat until the chicken is cooked through and is a rich golden color. Turn several times to brown evenly. Smoking time should be about 25 minutes.

Serve hot, or leave to cool and then slice thinly. Serve with mayonnaise and salad as a light luncheon dish.

Steam chicken on a rack or in bamboo basket

Add tea, orange rind and sugar to foil-lined wok

When smoking, place chicken on top of rack

Turn chicken several times to brown evenly

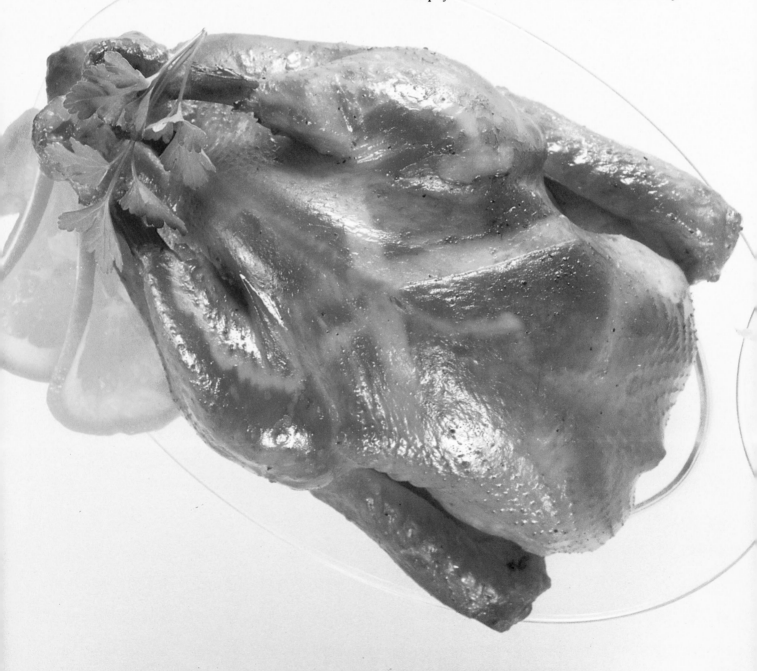

Duck Smoked with Camphor Wood* and Tea Leaves

SERVES 4

The elaborate carving of linen chests made from camphor wood has been a respected art in China for many centuries. And this craft has always yielded a ready source of chips and shavings of fragrant wood. Placed in the bottom of the wok, they impart a rich golden-red coloring and delicate smoky flavor, which combines particularly well with the rich taste of duck.

3 pounds duck
3 tablespoons Chinese black tea leaves
4 ounces camphor wood chips*
2 cups water

Wash the duck and wipe dry. Line the wok with a double thickness of aluminum foil and put in the tea leaves, wood chips and the water. Bring to a boil. Set a metal rack in the wok and place the duck on top. Cover and steam until the water has evaporated, then continue to cook for about 1¼ hours, turning the duck from time to time. After the water evaporates, the wood chips and tea leaves will dry out and begin to smoke, so the duck is cooked in a combination of steam and smoke—making it moist and aromatic and drawing out much of the excess fat.

*If unobtainable, hickory wood chips can be used.

Add water to tea leaves and wood in lined wok

Set duck on a metal rack over wood chip mixture

Chinese metal racks can be easily bent to desired height for greater convenience

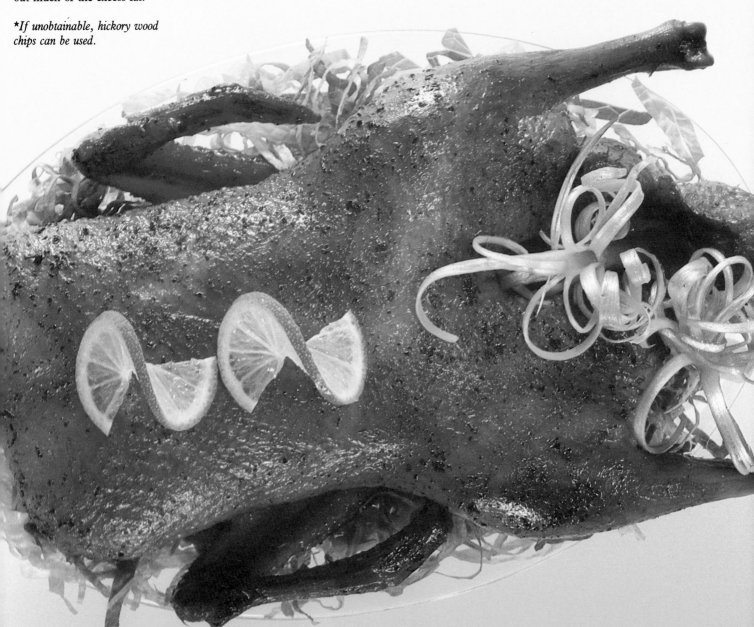

Rosemary-smoked Steaks

SERVES 4

4 sirloin or porterhouse steaks
3 tablespoons beef drippings or cooking oil
  and butter mixed
2 to 3 large sprigs fresh rosemary

Trim the steaks if necessary. Heat the fat in the wok and
quickly brown the steaks on both sides to seal and color.
Remove, then drain the wok and rinse.

Place the rosemary in the wok and set a rack over it.
Arrange the steaks on the rack. Cover the wok and smoke for
12 to 15 minutes until the steaks are cooked to individual taste.
Serve at once, garnished with rosemary.

The wok can also be used in conjunction with a barbecue
fire to make delectable grilled steaks with a smoky flavor.
Prepare a charcoal or wood-chip fire and allow it to burn
down to glowing coals. Set a rack over the fire and place the
steaks on top to sear quickly on both sides. Dampen branches
of fresh rosemary (or use handfuls of well-soaked hickory
chips) and place on the fire. Cover with an upside down wok
and allow the steaks to smoke until cooked to taste.

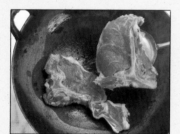

*Sear steaks, two at a time on
both sides*

*Place sprigs of rosemary in
foil-lined wok*

*Arrange steaks on a rack,
cover and smoke*

Smoked Rumpsteak

SERVES 6–8

A tasty and unusual main course, smoked beef is also a delicious appetizer.

3 pounds rump steak
1 tablespoon beef drippings or cooking oil
4 ounces hickory chips

Trim excess fat from the steak. Rub the wok with an oiled cloth, then heat the beef drippings or cooking oil. Sear the meat on all sides, then remove from the wok and rinse away the fat.

Line the interior of the wok with a double thickness of aluminum foil and put in the chips. Place the meat on a rack over the chips. Cover and set over high heat until the chips begin to smoke, then reduce the heat very slightly and continue to smoke for about 35 minutes, or until the meat is cooked to taste. A meat thermometer can be used to test if the meat is done. Remove from the wok and allow to cool slightly. Slice thinly and serve hot topped with fried onion rings and herbs, or cold with mayonnaise, horseradish or mustard.

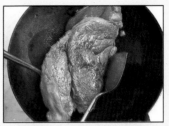

Sear the rump steak on both sides

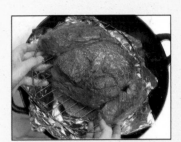

Place the meat on a rack over wood chips in foil-lined wok and cook over high heat

Smoked Fish

SERVES 4

This can be crisply deep-fried or eaten as it is.

4 fillets sea bass
3 tablespoons green tea leaves
2 tablespoons light soy sauce
2 teaspoons dry sherry or ginger wine
½ teaspoon Chinese spiced salt

Place the fish fillets on a smoking rack. Line the wok with a double thickness of aluminum foil and put in the tea leaves. Set the rack in place. Brush the fish with the soy sauce and sherry or wine on both sides. Cover the wok and smoke the fish for 10 minutes.

Serve straight from the pan with a soy sauce and spiced salt dip.

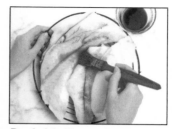

Brush fish fillets with soy sauce and wine

Fish will take about 10 minutes to smoke

Thai Smoked Crabs

SERVES 4

This is served at Thailand's island resorts. The fibrous outer husks from local coconuts are piled into a large drum, set on fire and then splashed with water to produce an aromatic smoke. Small sand or spider crabs are placed on wire mesh over the smoke and are permeated with a delicate smoky coconut flavor.

Set crabs on rack over wood chips

Crack crab claws with a cleaver before serving

4 small crabs
Coconut husks (or hickory chips)

Use a heavy cleaver to cut the husks into thin shreds. Line the wok with several layers of aluminum foil and put in the husks. Sprinkle on 1 to 2 tablespoons of water. Place a rack over the husks and set the whole crabs on top. Heat until smoking, cover the wok and smoke for about 20 minutes.

Crack the shells with the cleaver before serving. Delicious with icy cold beer and a chili sauce dip.

Smoked John Dory

SERVES 4–6

1 pound John Dory (halibut or cod can be substituted)
1 tablespoon dry sherry
½ teaspoon salt
3 tablespoons light soy sauce
2 teaspoons sugar
2 tablespoons spring onion, finely chopped
2 teaspoons fresh gingerroot, grated
3 tablespoons Chinese black tea leaves
2 tablespoons sugar

Clean and wash the fish and wipe dry. Score deeply in several places on each side, then place in a dish. Mix the sherry, salt, soy sauce, sugar, onion and ginger together. Rub over the fish, then cover with a piece of plastic wrap and leave for at least 1 hour to absorb the flavors.

Line the inside of a wok with a double thickness of aluminum foil and put in the tea leaves and sugar. Set a rack over this and heat until the leaves begin to smoke.

Drain the fish and wipe with paper towels. Place on the rack, cover the wok and smoke over moderate heat until the fish is cooked through and is a rich golden color (about 25 minutes), turning once or twice.

Remove from the wok and brush lightly with sesame or cooking oil to give the skin a shine. Serve with mayonnaise.

Cucumbers and radishes, sliced and pickled in a mixture of white vinegar, sugar and salt for about 2 hours, make a tasty accompaniment to this dish.

Rub flavorings over the scored John Dory

Line a wok with foil, add tea leaves and sugar

Tabletop Cooking

Cooking at the table produces a distinct ambience at a dinner party. It can introduce a note of informality, or charge the occasion with a feeling of super-sophistication. It can highlight the skills of a talented amateur chef, or disguise the insecurities of the host who does not want to rely on his limited ability in the kitchen.

An elegant flambé, prepared at the table and served as the prelude to the meal, perhaps to be followed by an oven-cooked main course and a simple dessert or cheese, would make an impressive menu. Yet the host could be there at the dinner table with his guests throughout the meal, instead of finding himself with little more than a few minutes to chat and eat between excursions to the kitchen.

One-pot meals such as the Japanese *Sukiyaki* or *Tempura* can be cooked at the table; they look spectacular and taste superb, and guests can participate freely in the cooking and serving. They bring to the table a casual, even intimate atmosphere, which should allow conversation to flow and friendships to blossom.

Few hosts want to spend time in the kitchen preparing a hot dessert. Yet on many occasions something hot, full of rich flavors and laced with liqueurs is needed to round off a menu. A tabletop dessert of flambéed fruits, a sweet omelette or crêpes cooked at the table and wrapped around prepared fruit and cream fillings are dishes that are easy on the chef and bring the dinner party to a dramatic conclusion.

There are a number of different types of portable cookers—ranging from the small electric type with a dish-shaped ring curved to accommodate a wok, to one-ring gas cookers especially made to work with a wok. These may need to be dressed up to improve their appearance for use on the table, and for this a "skirt" of aluminum foil may be the answer. Remember too that they may become hot underneath, so place them on a thick cutting board to prevent spoiling your tabletop.

For even more convenience, use an electric wok for tabletop cooking. It can stand directly on the table without causing heat damage, is light and is easily portable, which means that it does not need to be set up in advance but simply brought to the table when required, plugged in, and you're ready to begin.

Food to be cooked at the table should be completely prepared in advance and arranged attractively on platters. Place these near the cooker and have the required cooking utensils—the wok "charn," a pair of tongs, a tasting spoon and a metal ladle for heating liquor for flambéeing—on a tray or cloth nearby. Plates or a serving platter should be warmed and ready as well.

Tabletop meals at which guests participate in the cooking require careful organization to ensure that all have access to the uncooked food, the wok and the necessary seasonings and utensils. Depending on the number of guests, seating configuration and the size of your table, divide the uncooked ingredients evenly between several plates and place these at even intervals around the table. Have jars and bowls of seasonings, and an adequate number of the required cooking utensils grouped near the wok.

If there are more than half a dozen guests, or if the table is a long one, it will be necessary to organize two separate cooking areas. This can be done without loss of the easy spirit that should go hand in hand with cook-it-yourself meals.

Tempura

SERVES 4 AS A MAIN COURSE,
6–8 AS AN APPETIZER

The ideal way to cook *Tempura* is right there at the table, as it must come straight from the pan to be at its very best. Cover a corner of the table with a cloth, preferably plastic, and set up a portable wok or an electric wok filled with clean cooking oil. The Japanese use long thin metal chopsticks for retrieving the cooked *Tempura* from the hot oil, but wooden cooking chopsticks or tongs will do just as well.

1 green or red pepper
1 small sweet potato
1 large onion
8 spring onions
8 French beans
3 fillets sea perch or similar fish
3 fresh squid
8 medium raw shrimp
2 teaspoons dry sherry or
   ginger wine
Pinch of salt

Batter
2 cups flour
½ cup cornstarch
2 medium eggs, beaten
2 cups water

Sauce
1 cup Japanese dashi stock*
½ cup light soy sauce
½ cup sweet sherry
3 tablespoons finely grated white radish
   or Japanese daikon

Trim away the seed core, stem and inner ribs of the pepper and cut it into small squares. Peel and slice the sweet potato and onion. Trim the spring onions and beans but leave whole. Cut the fish into fingers and the squid into rings. Devein the shrimp, leaving the tails on, and marinate with the sherry or wine, and the salt. Arrange the vegetables and seafood attractively on a large platter.

Beat the batter ingredients together. The batter should be of the consistency of lightly whipped cream. Do not overbeat, as tiny lumps are acceptable in a *Tempura* batter.

Mix the sauce ingredients together and pour into a small bowl for each guest.

When ready to serve, heat the oil to hot. Dip the ingredients into the batter and deep-fry until crisp and cooked through. Cook each different ingredient separately and serve directly onto your guests' plates. The sauce is used as a dip.

If dashi cannot be found at a Chinese or Japanese food store, substitute chicken stock made with a stock cube or powder and add about 3 tablespoons of orange juice to give an equally tasty sauce.

*Prepare vegetables and
arrange on a platter*

*Arrange seafood
attractively on a platter*

*Ingredients may be
skewered, then battered*

Sizzling Sesame Beef

SERVES 4

1 pound beef fillet or rump steak
½ teaspoon crushed garlic
2 tablespoons dry sherry
1 tablespoon sesame oil
2 tablespoons dark soy sauce
2 teaspoons sugar
2 teaspoons cornstarch
1 medium onion
2 tablespoons vegetable or peanut oil
2 teaspoons sesame seeds

Sauce
⅓ cup water
2 teaspoons dry sherry
1 tablespoon light soy sauce
1 teaspoon cornstarch

Partially freeze the beef so that it is more easily cut into paper-thin slices. Place in a dish with the garlic, sherry, sesame oil, soy sauce, sugar and cornstarch. Mix well and leave for 1 to 2 hours to marinate.

Peel and halve the onion and cut it into thin wedges. Separate each slice and set aside. Mix the sauce ingredients together in a small bowl.

Heat the wok at the table. Add the vegetable or peanut oil and put in the onion and sesame seeds. Sauté until the sesame seeds are golden, then remove.

Wipe out the wok, reheat the oil and add the beef. Sauté on high heat until just cooked (about 2½ minutes). Return the onion and sesame seeds, and pour in the sauce. Simmer briskly until the sauce thickens, then serve.

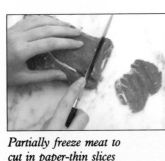

Partially freeze meat to cut in paper-thin slices

Cut onions into wedges and separate

Pepper Steaks

SERVES 6

6 fillet or rump steaks
¼ cup butter
1 tablespoon cooking oil
1 tablespoon flour
½ cup dry white wine
1 tablespoon brandy
½ cup beef stock
Pinch of sugar
1 tablespoon black peppercorns, lightly crushed
1 tablespoon canned green peppercorns, drained
3 tablespoons heavy cream

Trim the steaks if necessary. Assemble the ingredients at the table.

Heat the wok to moderate and add the butter and oil. Fry the steaks quickly on each side, then cook until done to taste. Remove and keep warm.

Sprinkle the flour into the wok and stir in lightly, then add the wine and bring to a boil. Simmer briefly. Heat the brandy in a metal ladle, ignite and pour into the wok. Add the beef stock and boil for about 3 minutes. Add the sugar and peppercorns, reduce the heat and simmer for 2 to 3 minutes. Add the cream and heat through. Serve the steaks with a generous amount of the sauce.

Brown steaks in butter and oil, turn with 2 spoons

Heat brandy in metal ladle and ignite

Sukiyaki

SERVES 4 GENEROUSLY

Sukiyaki was probably the first Japanese dish to achieve recognition and acceptance in Western households, and it remains a popular dinner party feature. It is easy to prepare, fun to cook and eat, and is ideal for impromptu dinners.

1½ pounds sirloin or porterhouse steak,
   in one piece
4 squares soft bean curd (tofu)*
2 medium onions
8 spring onions
2 bunches watercress
8 dried Japanese black mushrooms, soaked
6 ounces shiritaki noodles or Chinese "glass"
   noodles, or mung bean vermicelli
2 to 3 pieces fresh beef suet
4 eggs

Sauce
1 cup light soy sauce
1¼ cups Japanese dashi stock★★
½ cup sake (rice wine) or Japanese mirin (sweet rice
   wine)
3½ tablespoons sugar

Trim the steak and cut into very thin slices. This can be done more easily if the meat has been partially frozen beforehand to make it firm. Arrange the meat on one or two platters.

Cut the bean curd into small cubes and place with the meat. Peel and slice the onions. Trim the spring onions and leave whole. Rinse the vegetables and shake off excess water. Drain the mushrooms when softened and remove the stems; cut a cross in the top of each to decorate it and to allow it to cook quicker. Drop the noodles into boiling water to soften, then drain well. Mix the sauce ingredients together in a bowl.

When ready to cook, set up an electric or portable wok in the center of the table on a cloth. Heat the wok and rub the suet over the bottom until well greased.

Hand each diner a fresh egg, to be beaten in his or her own bowl. This will be used as a dip, in conjunction with some of the prepared sauce.

Bring the meat platter and the other ingredients to the table, placing them within easy reach of the diners. Hand each person a pair of wooden chopsticks.

Fry the meat quickly, then splash on a little of the sauce for flavor. Cook portions of the remaining ingredients separately in the center, until done to taste, adding plenty of the sauce. The diners help themselves to meat, vegetables and noodles, dipping them into the egg and sauce before eating.

*If tofu is not available, or not appreciated, peel and slice a sweet potato and cut a red or green pepper into squares to substitute.

**If dashi is unobtainable, use chicken stock powder mixed with water and add ½ cup of orange juice.

Cube the tofu (bean curd)

Cut a cross on soaked mushrooms

Soak noodles in boiling water to soften

Cook portions of sukiyaki at the table

Sweet Omelette with Strawberry Sauce

SERVES 6

Easier than a soufflé and just as tasty, sweet omelettes garnished with fruity sauces are popular in northern European countries.

8 eggs
3 tablespoons milk
2 teaspoons cornstarch
1 tablespoon sugar
1 tablespoon unsalted butter
1 tablespoon brandy or Kirsch

Strawberry Sauce
1 pint fresh strawberries★
1 cup sweet white wine
1 tablespoon lemon juice
1 tablespoon sugar
1 tablespoon flour
2 tablespoons butter

Prepare the sauce first. Hull the strawberries, rinse and dry, then cut into halves. Set aside. Bring the remaining sauce ingredients to a boil in a saucepan or wok and whisk briskly to incorporate the flour and sugar. When thickened, remove from the heat, add the strawberries and keep warm until needed.

Beat 5 eggs and the yolks of the remaining eggs together, adding the milk, cornstarch and sugar. Beat the egg whites separately to soft peaks, then carefully fold into the batter.

Melt the butter in the wok at the table. Pour in the batter and cook, covered, over moderate heat until the omelette is lightly browned and beginning to firm up.

Fold in half and continue to cook, covered, until the inside is just firm. If the underside begins to get too brown, flip the folded pancake over and continue to cook gently. Make sure the heat isn't too high.

Use two spatulas to carefully lift the omelette onto a serving dish. Pour on the prepared strawberry sauce. Heat the brandy or Kirsch in a metal ladle and ignite. Pour over the dessert and serve at once with whipped cream.

★*This omelette is equally delicious served with drained, canned, stoned black cherries.*

Fold whisked egg whites into yolk mixture

Pour into melted butter in wok

Cherries Jubilee

SERVES 4

1 can stoned black cherries in syrup
3 tablespoons butter
3 tablespoons brandy
1 tablespoon Kirsch
2 teaspoons cornstarch

Drain the cherries, reserving the syrup. Melt the butter in the wok at the table and sauté the cherries for about 1 minute, then pour in the brandy and ignite. Stir until the flames are extinguished, then add the Kirsch and boil briskly. Mix the cornstarch with three-quarters of the reserved cherry syrup and pour over the cherries. Stir on moderate heat until thickened. Serve on vanilla ice cream.

Sauté drained cherries in butter

Stir cornstarch with cherry juice, then add to wok

Tropical Fruit Flambé

SERVES 4

4 slices canned pineapple
1 ripe but firm banana
1 passionfruit
3 tablespoons butter
3½ tablespoons brown sugar
3 tablespoons fresh lime juice
3 tablespoons pineapple juice
2 tablespoons brandy
2 teaspoons dark rum
Whipped cream

Drain the pineapple. Peel the banana and cut in half lengthwise, then in half again to give four pieces. Open the passionfruit and set aside.

Heat the wok and melt the butter. Add the pineapple and banana and sauté gently until the banana is beginning to soften. Sprinkle on the brown sugar, then add the juices. Heat the brandy and rum together in a metal ladle and then ignite. Pour into the pan and boil briefly. Transfer the fruit to dessert dishes and top with whipped cream. Decorate with the passionfruit juice and seeds, and serve.

Cut halved banana into four pieces

Heat brandy and rum in a ladle and ignite

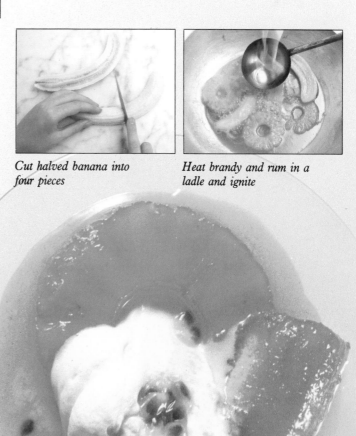

Index